trace
THE EMBROIDERED ART OF MICHELE CARRAGHER

trace

THE EMBROIDERED ART OF MICHELE CARRAGHER

Search Press

First published in 2021

Search Press Limited
Wellwood, North Farm Road,
Tunbridge Wells, Kent TN2 3DR

Text copyright © Michele Carragher 2021

Photographs by Michele Carragher and SJG Flockhart

Photographs copyright © Michele Carragher 2021, with the exception of photographs otherwise detailed

Design copyright © Search Press Ltd. 2021

All rights reserved. No part of this book, text, photographs or illustrations may be reproduced or transmitted in any form or by any means by print, photoprint, microfilm, microfiche, photocopier, internet or in any way known or as yet unknown, or stored in a retrieval system, without written permission obtained beforehand from Search Press. Printed in China.

ISBN: 978-1-78221-743-5
ebook ISBN: 978-1-78126-692-2

You are invited to visit the author's website:
www.michelecarragherembroidery.com

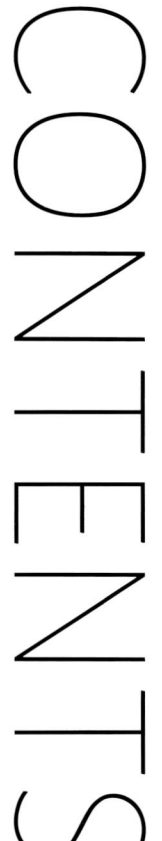

CONTENTS

TRACE: THE ARTWORKS	6
ALL THAT GLITTERS...	8
ENTROPY	20
CONSCIENCE	44
THE ARTIST'S INSIGHT	54
ARTEFACT INSIGHT: THE HAND	60
ARTWORK INSIGHT: ALL THAT GLITTERS...	78
ARTEFACT INSIGHT: THE HEART	92
ARTWORK INSIGHT: ENTROPY	106
ARTEFACT INSIGHT: THE HEAD	122
ARTWORK INSIGHT: CONSCIENCE	132
COSTUME EMBROIDERY	142
MY PATH INTO COSTUME WORK	144

TRACE: THE

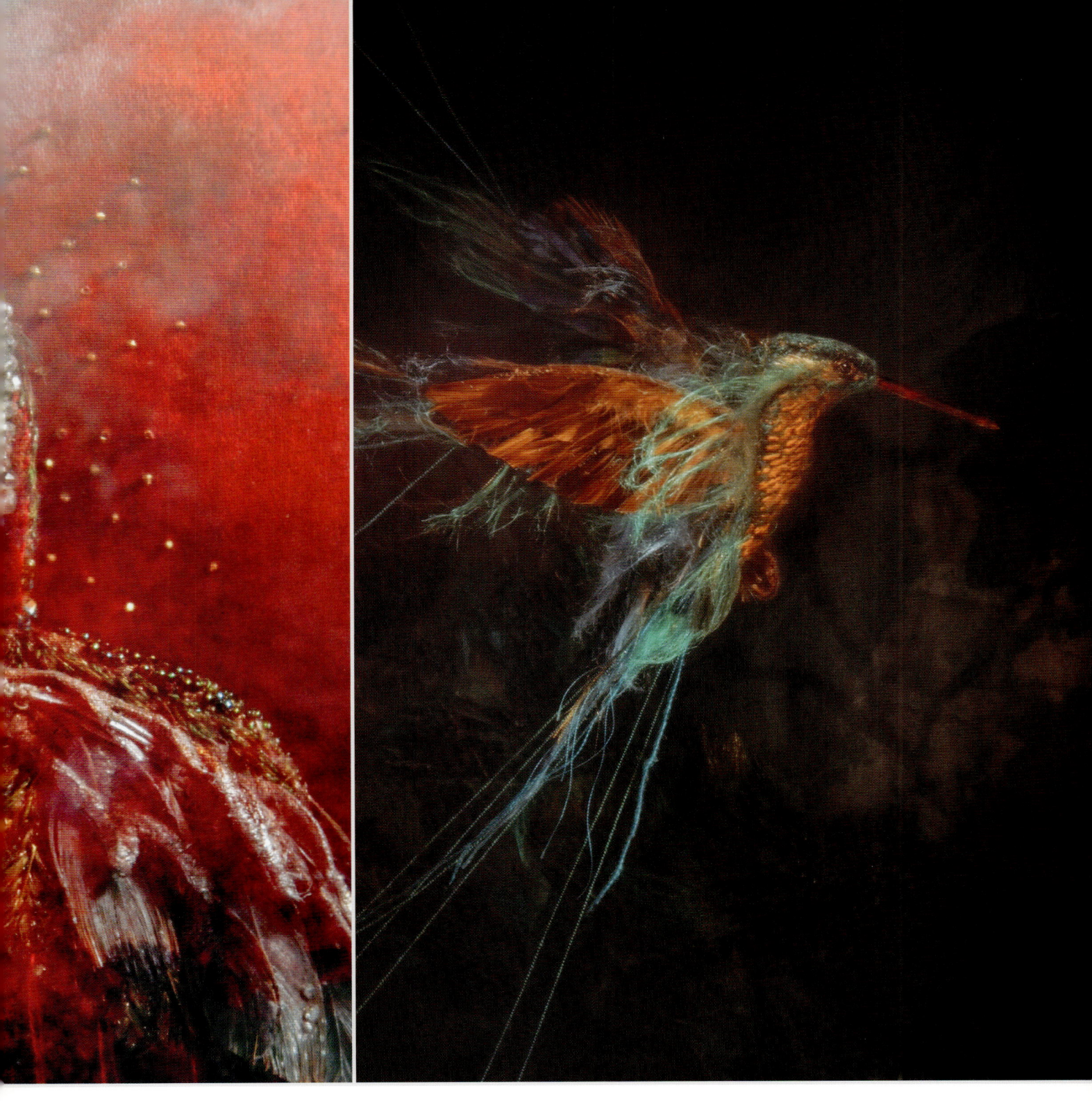

ARTWORKS

all that glitters...

"Harmony makes small things grow.
Lack of it makes big things decay."
Gaius Sallustius Crispus (Sallust)

entropy

*"... wealth is like sea-water; the more we drink,
the thirstier we become."*
Arthur Schopenhauer

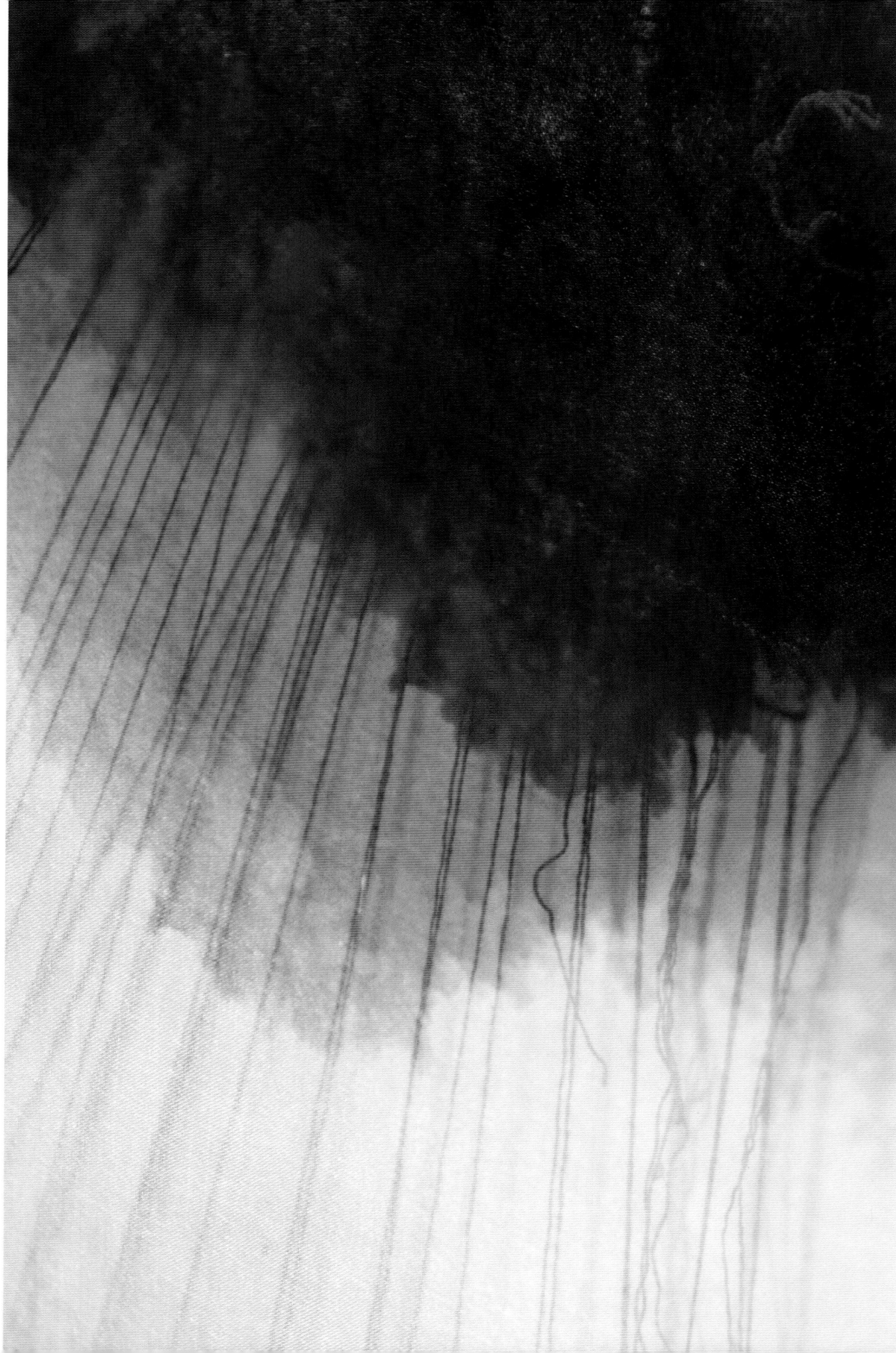

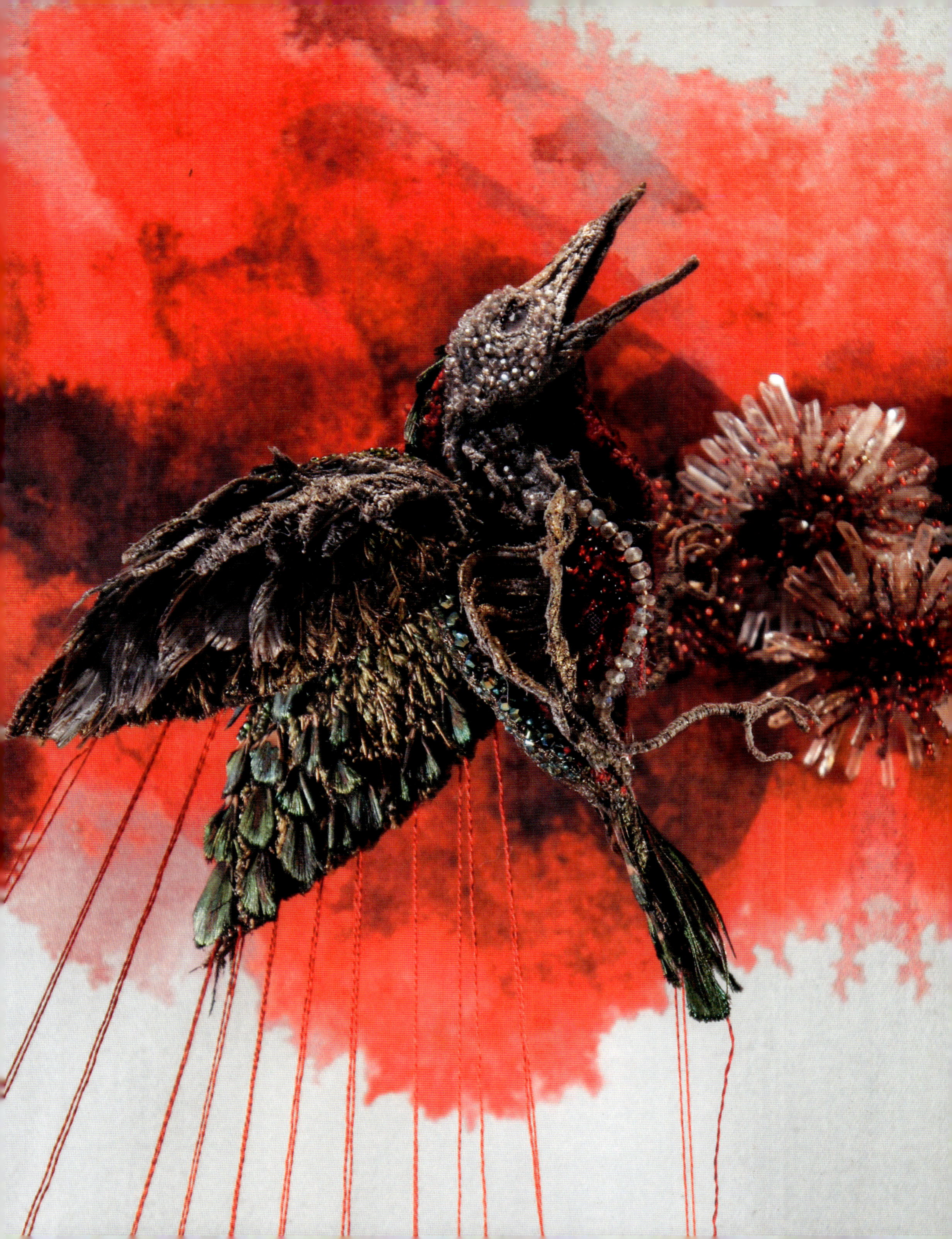

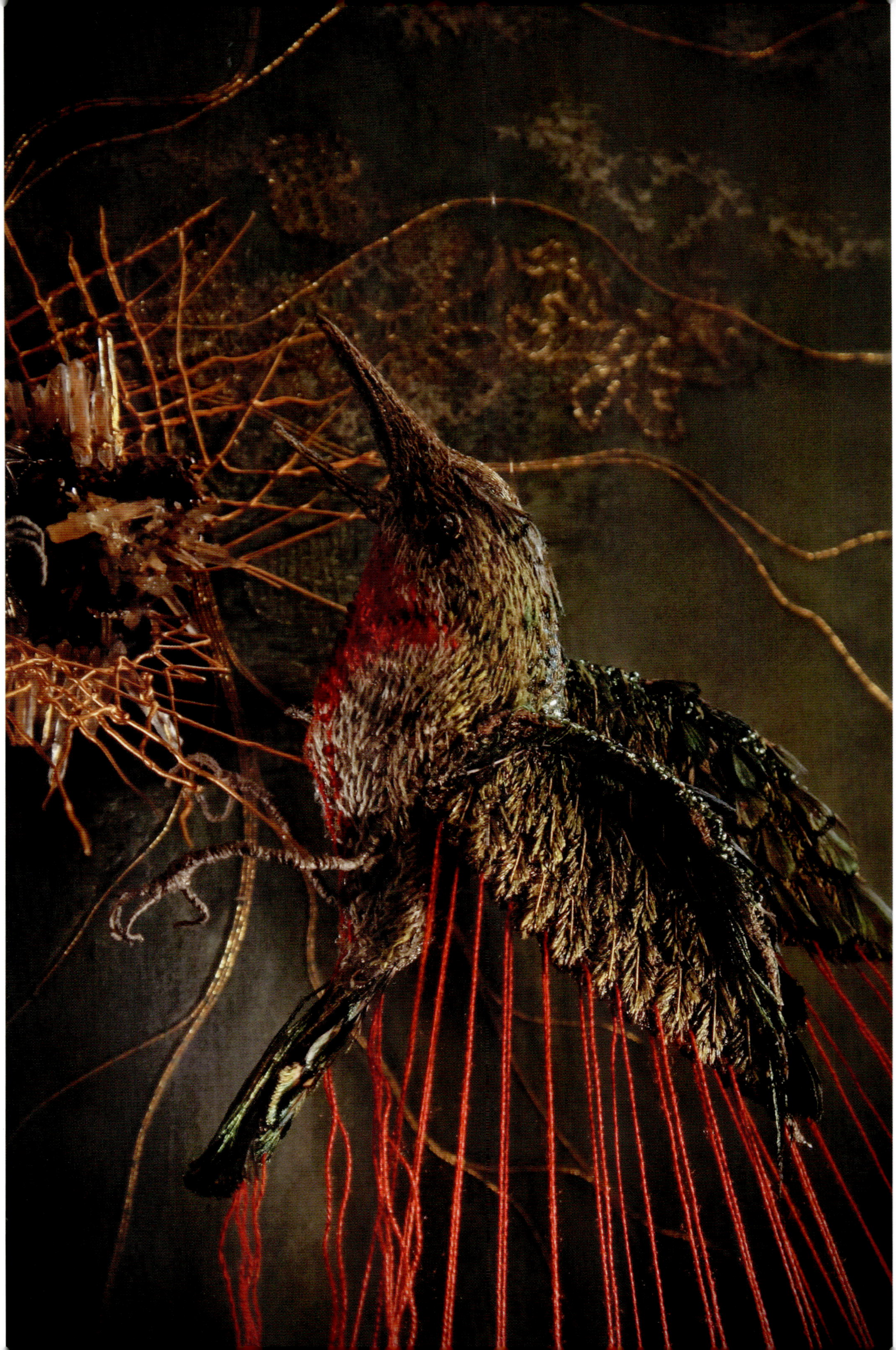

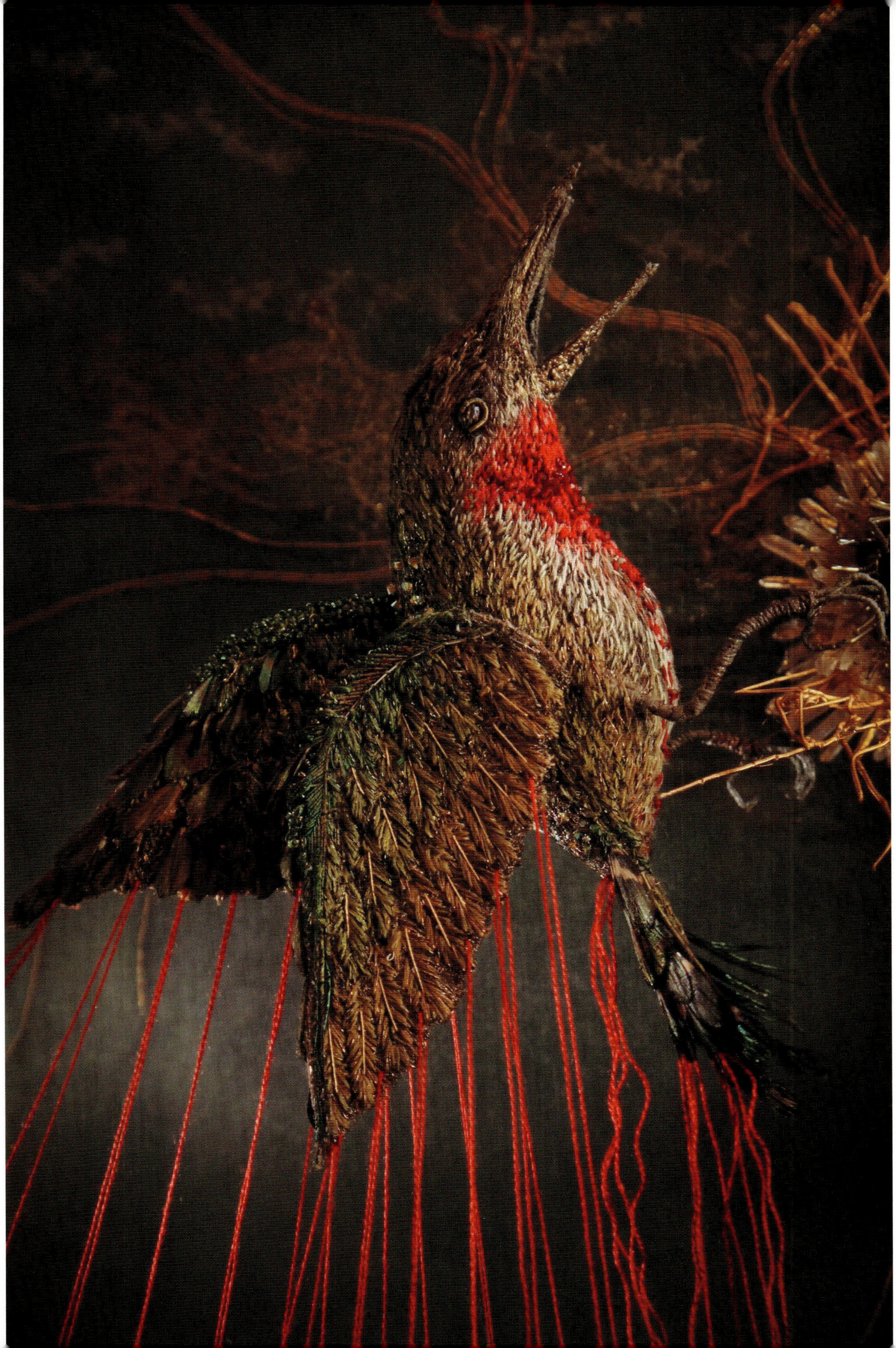

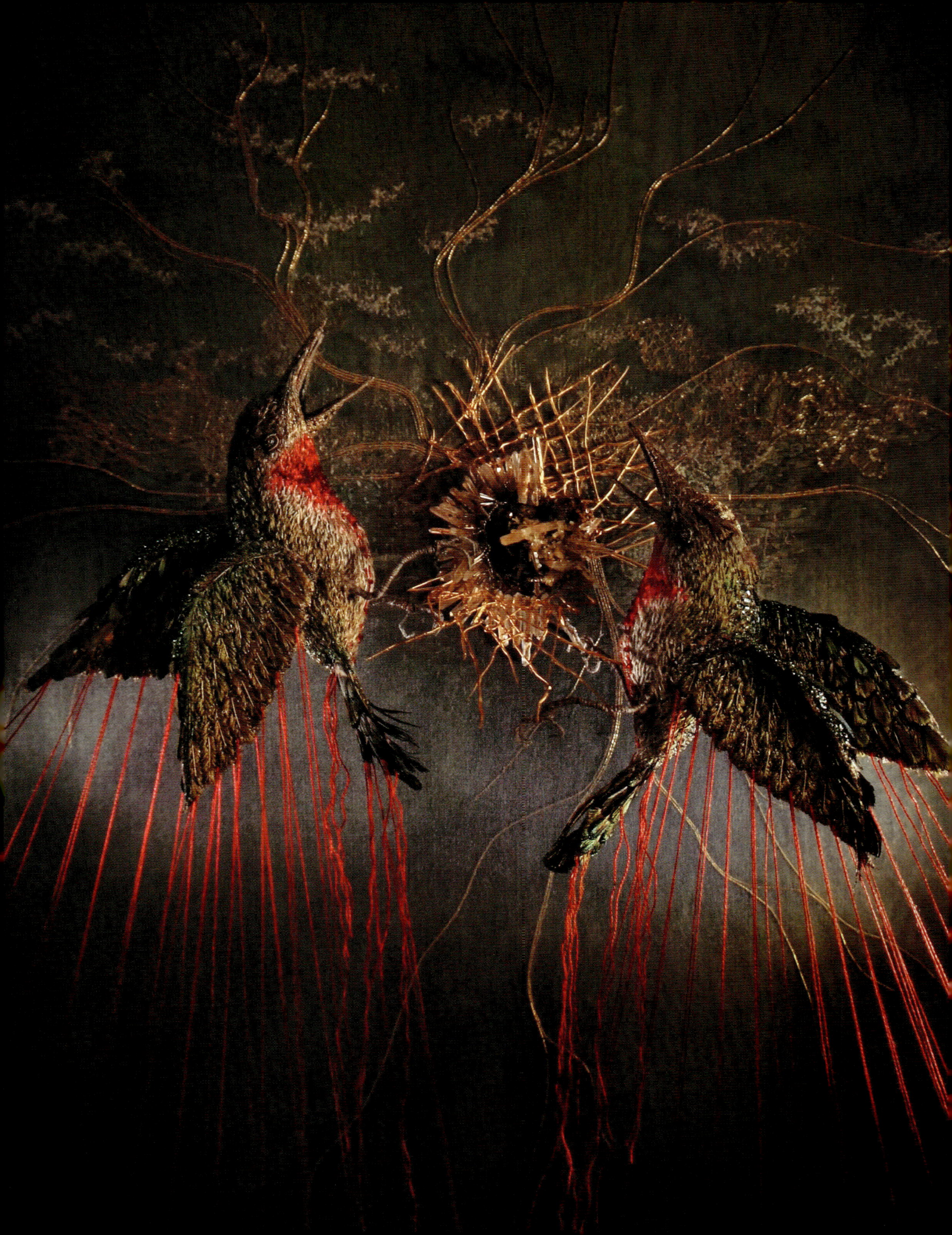

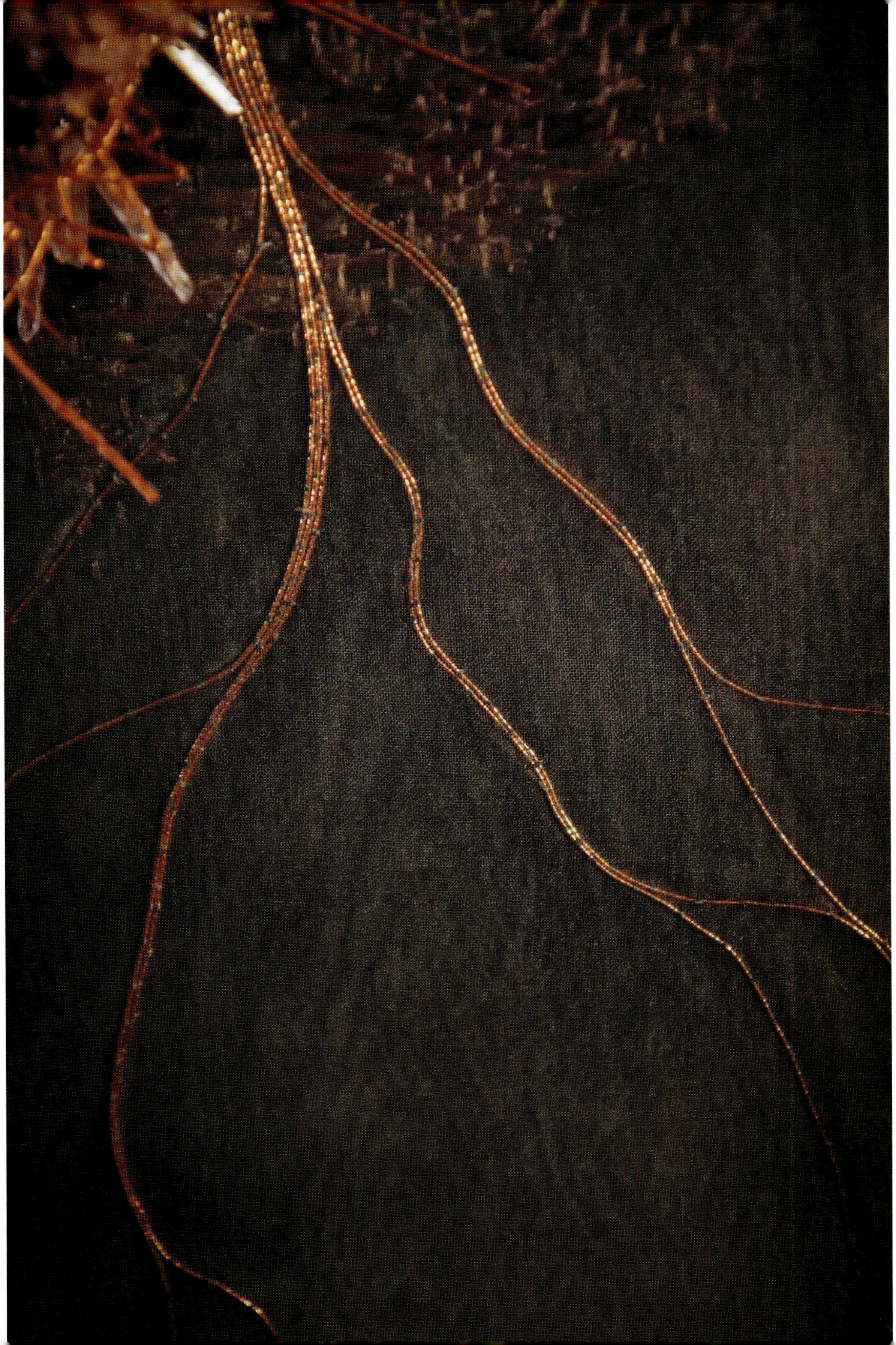

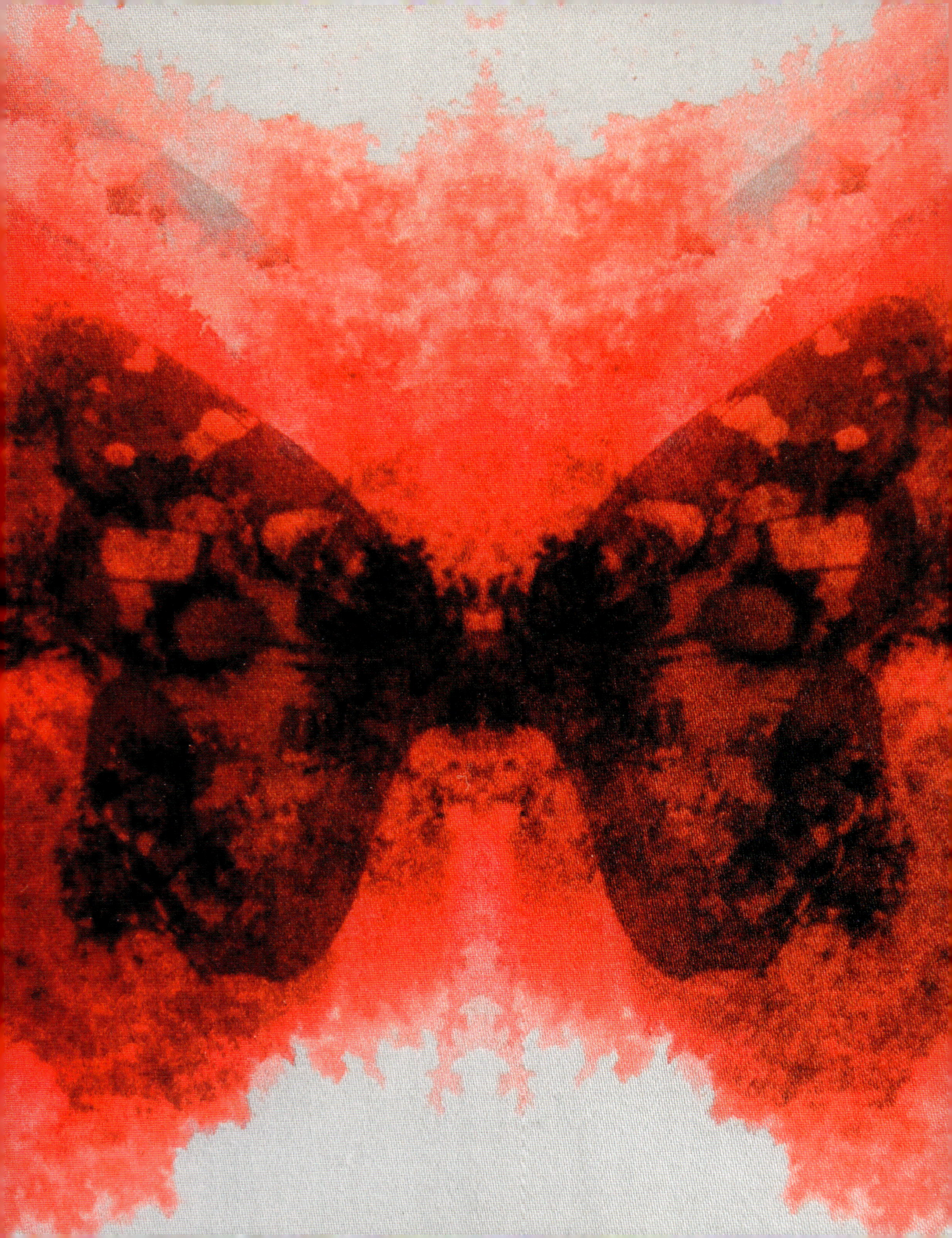

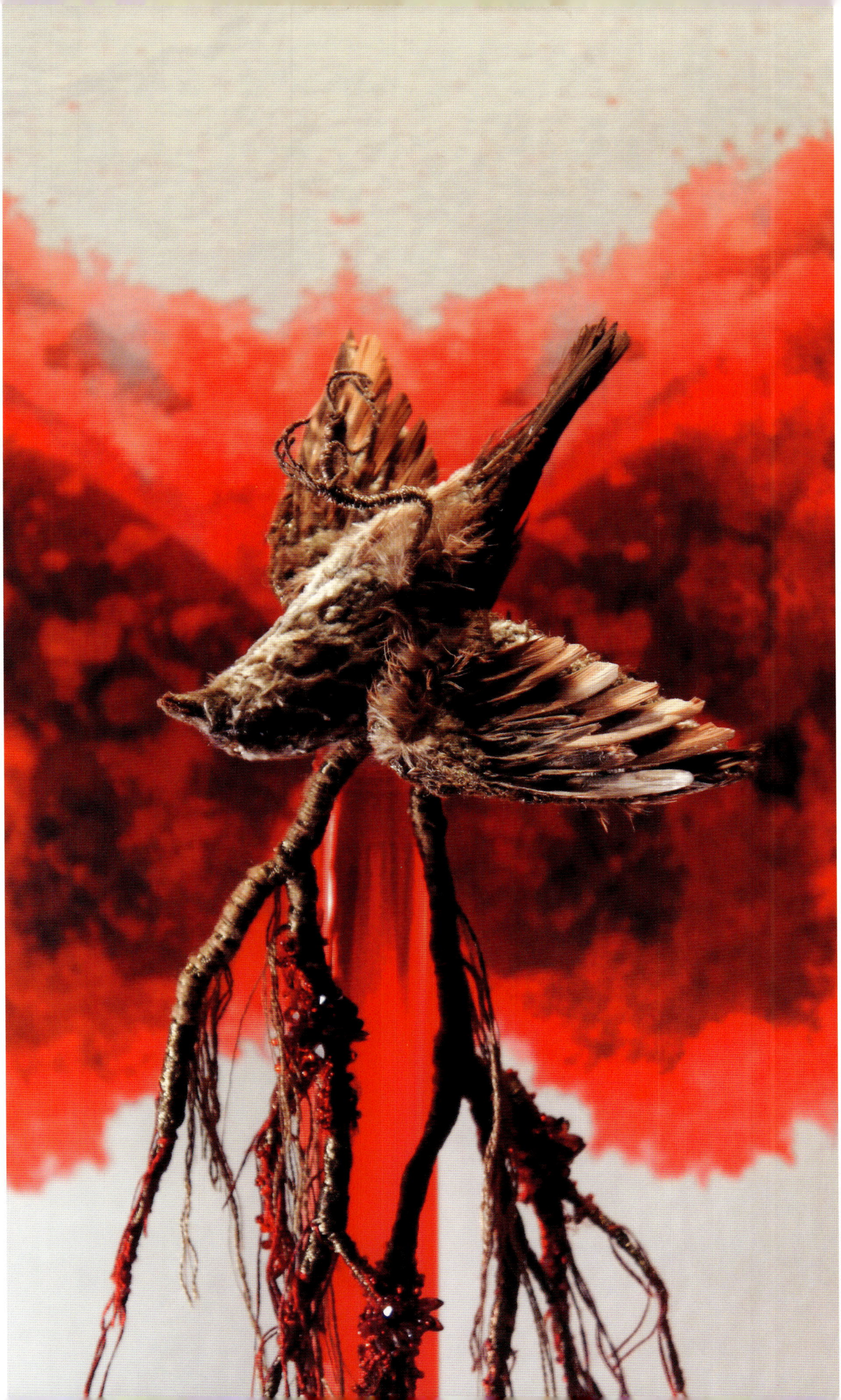

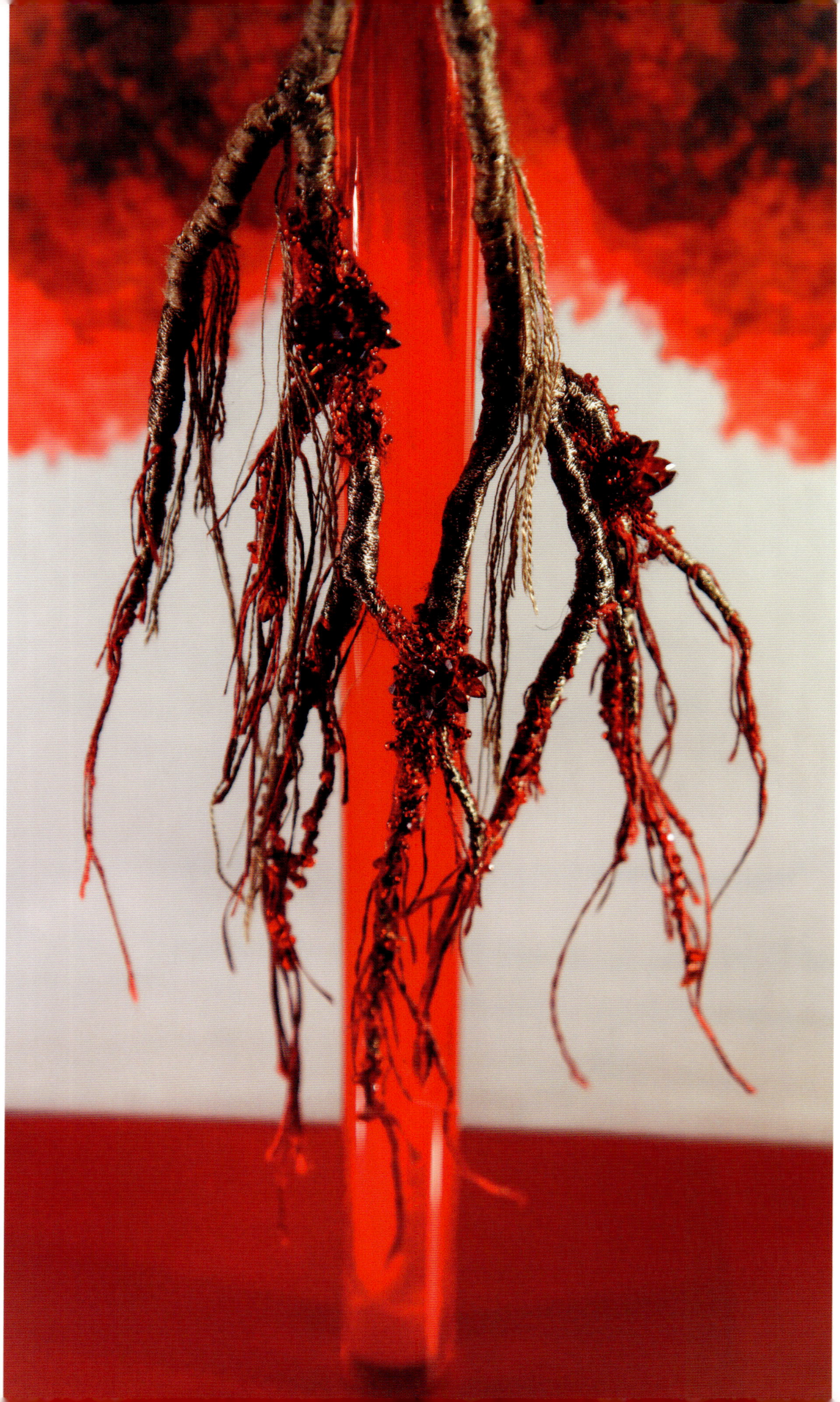

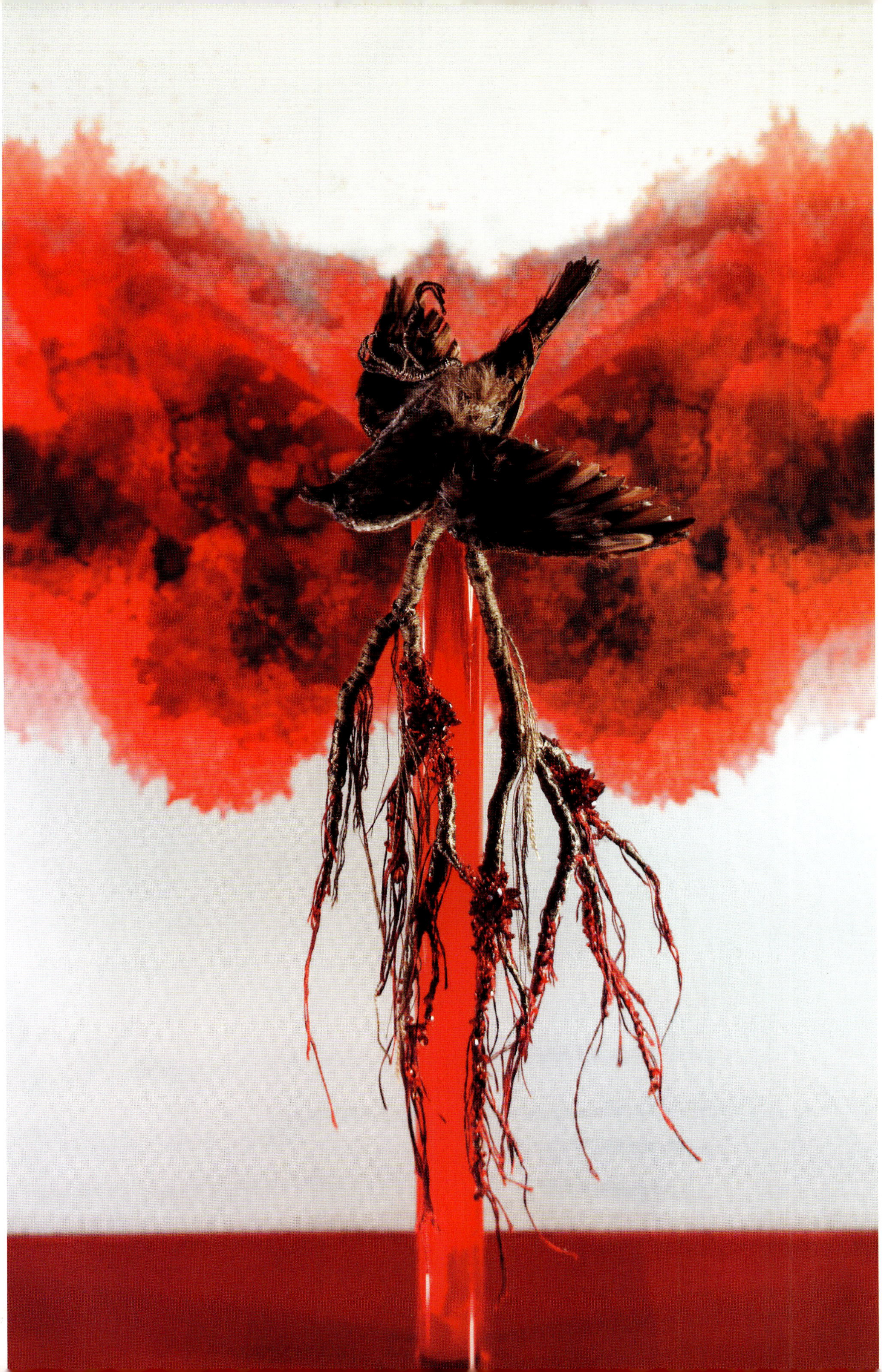

conscience

"What wisdom can you find that is greater than kindness?"
Jean-Jacques Rousseau

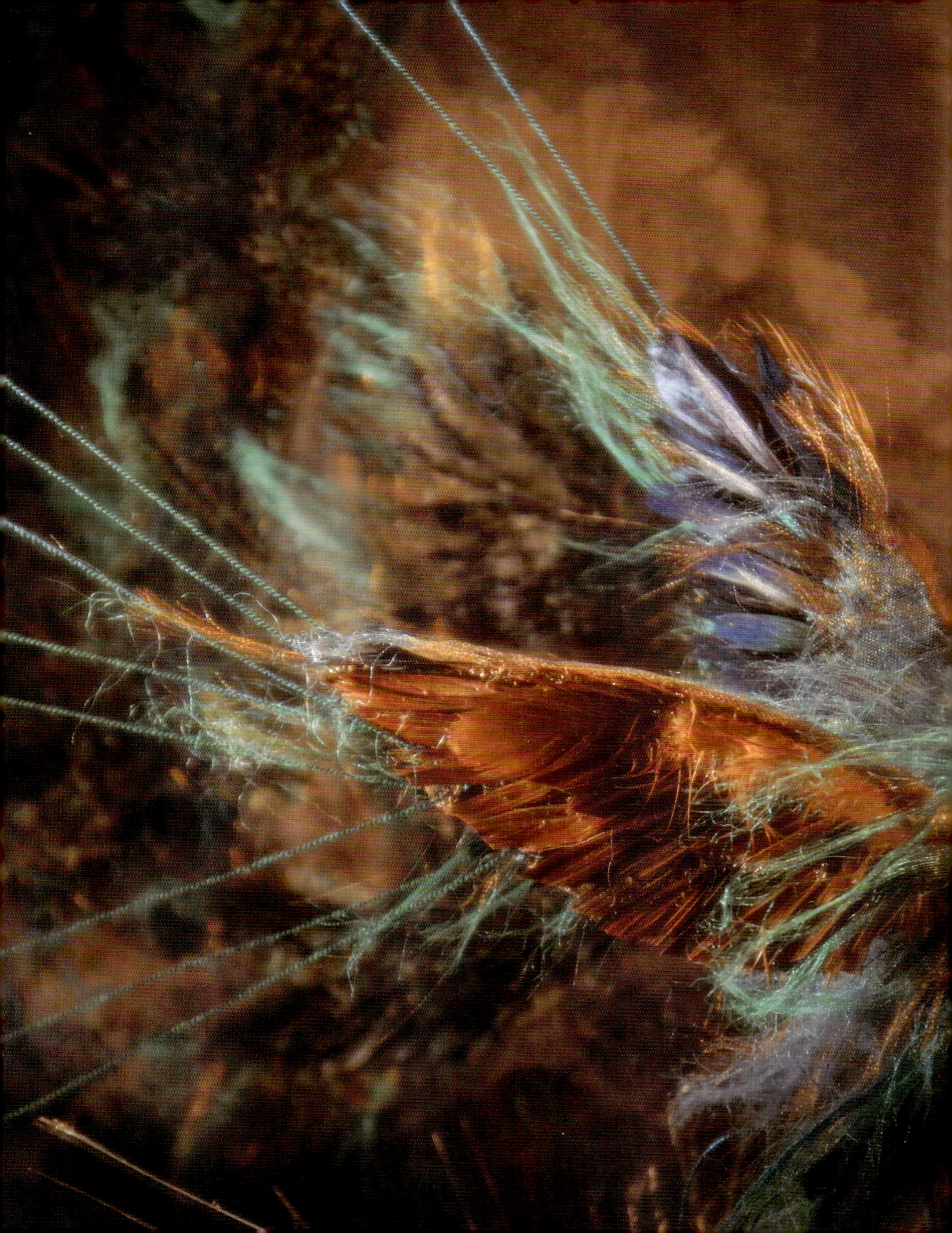

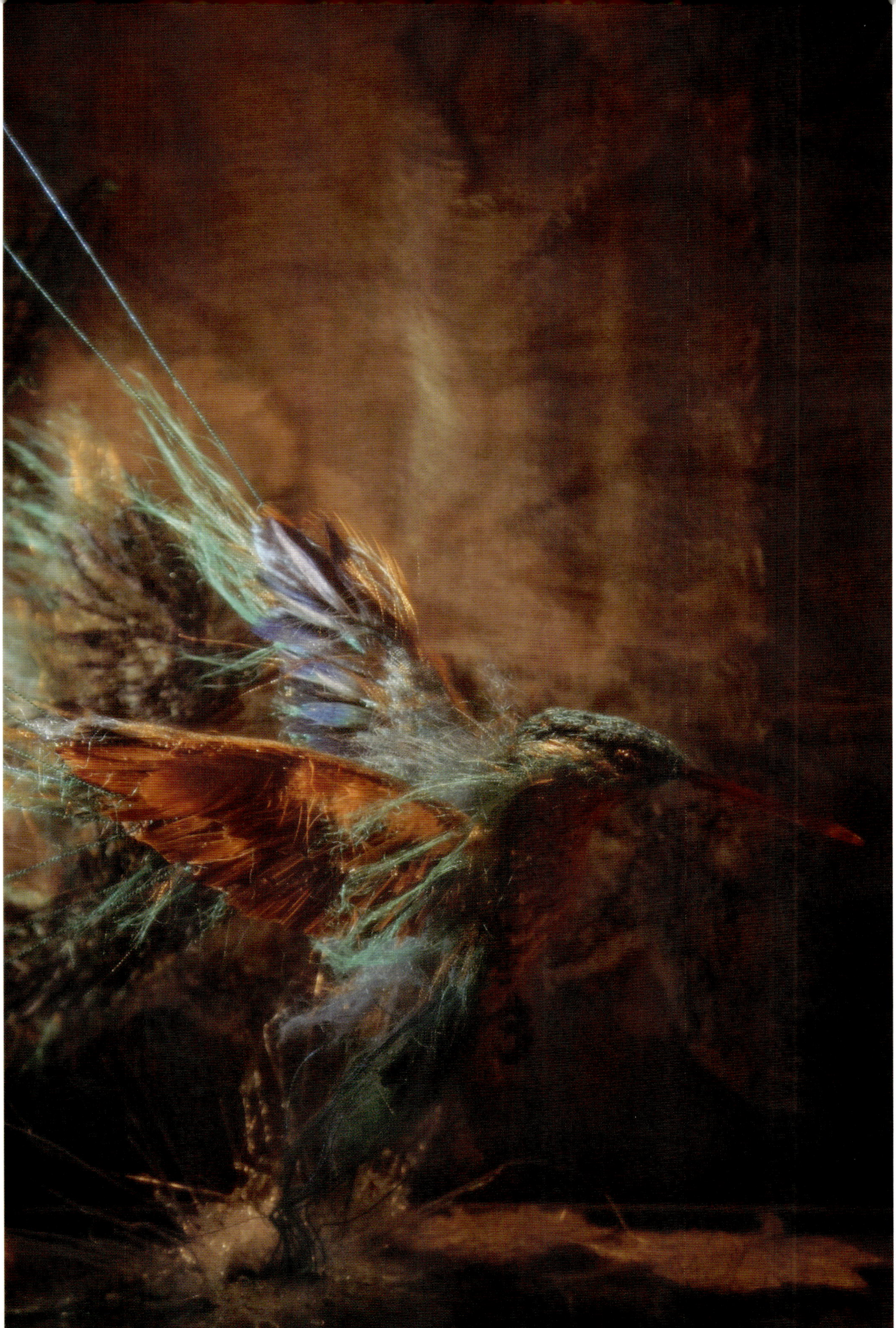

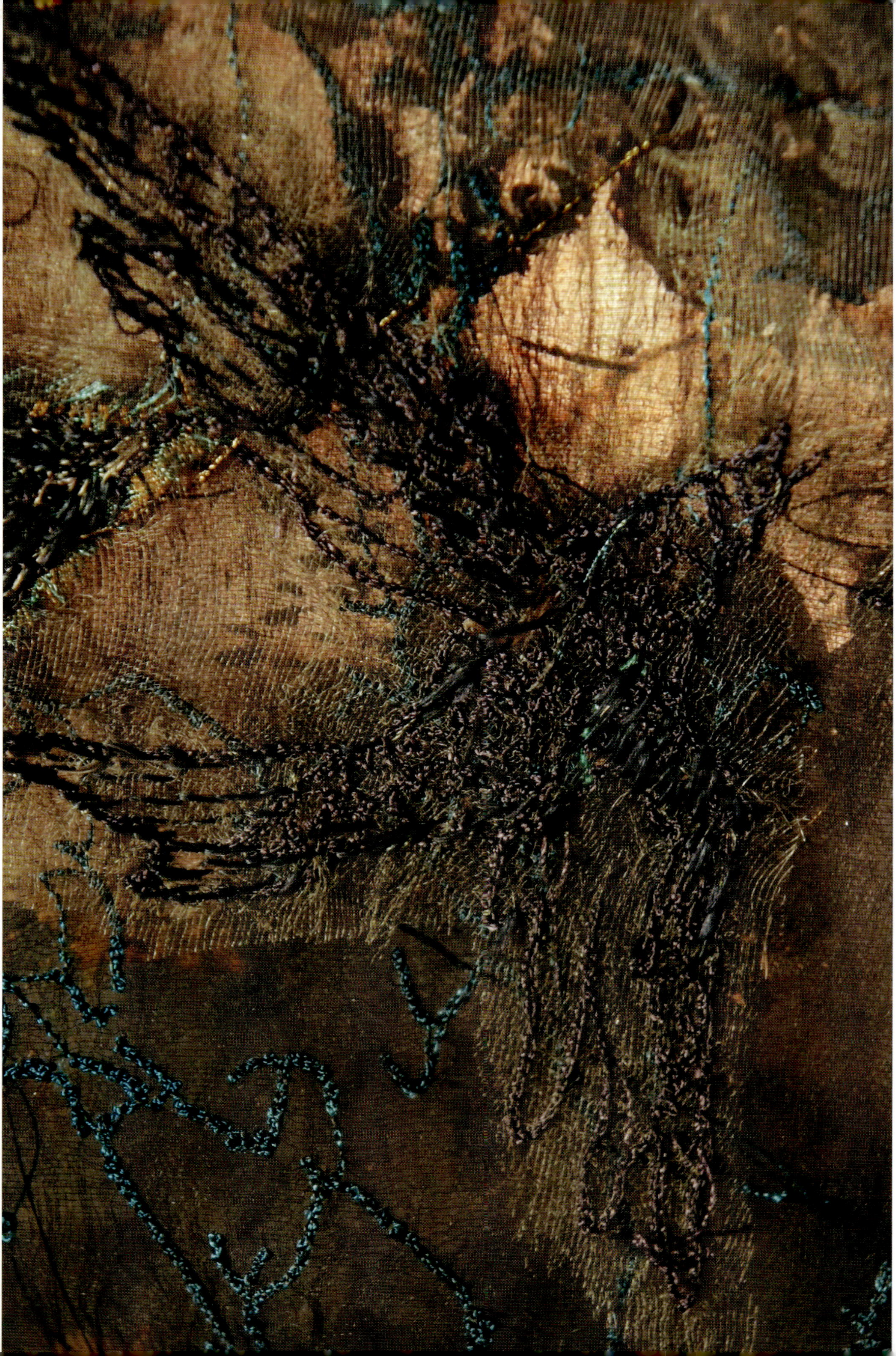

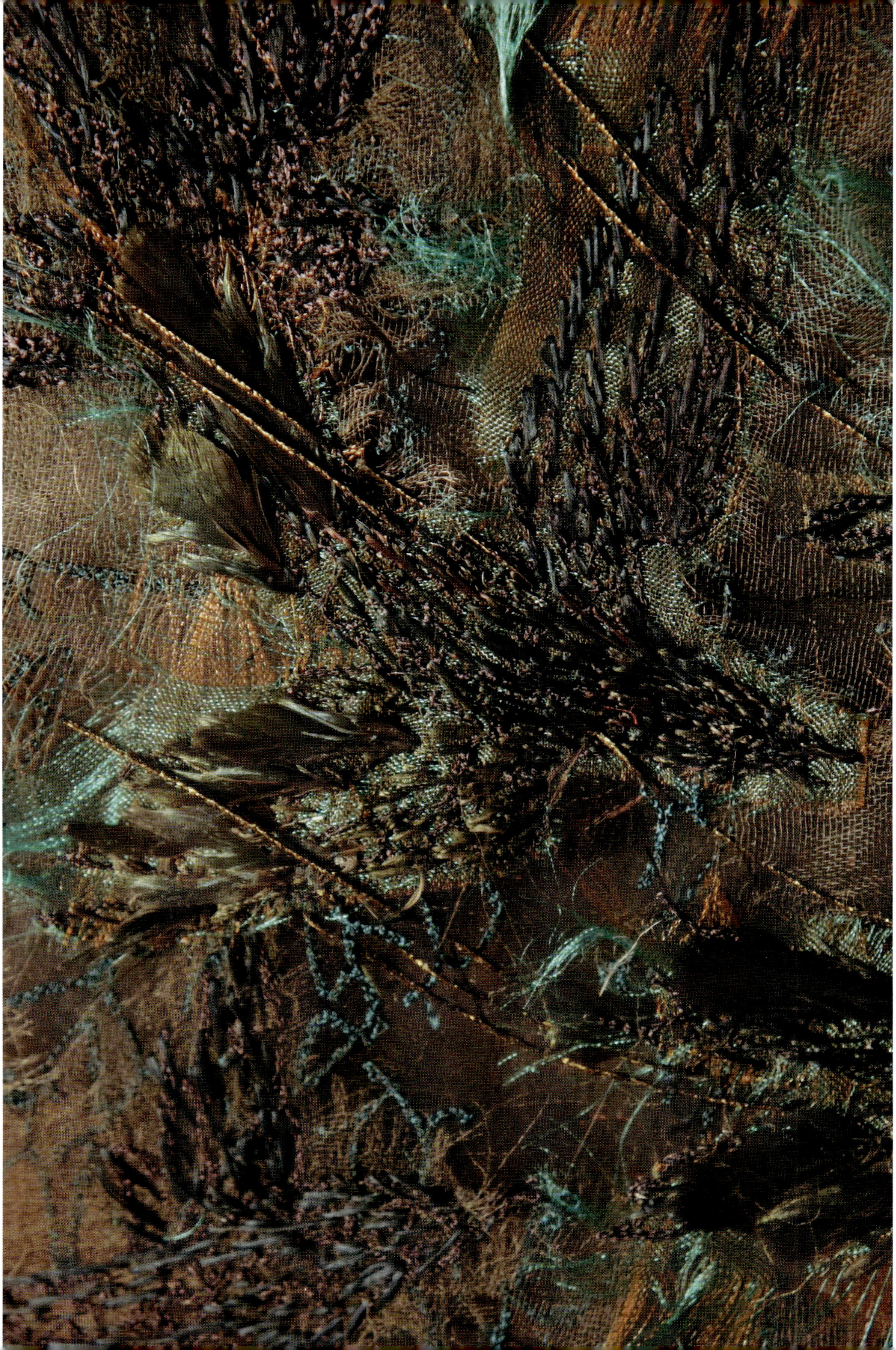

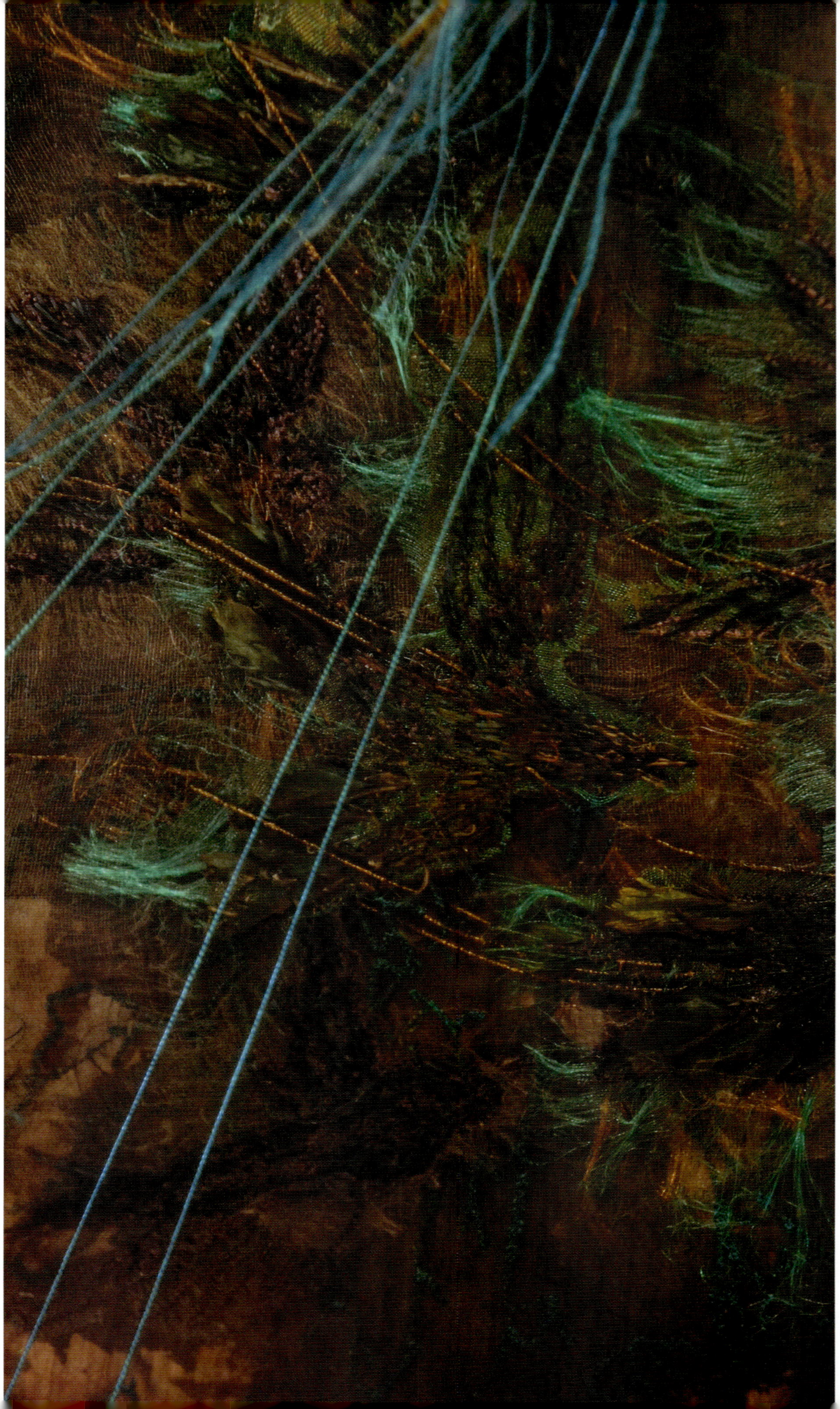

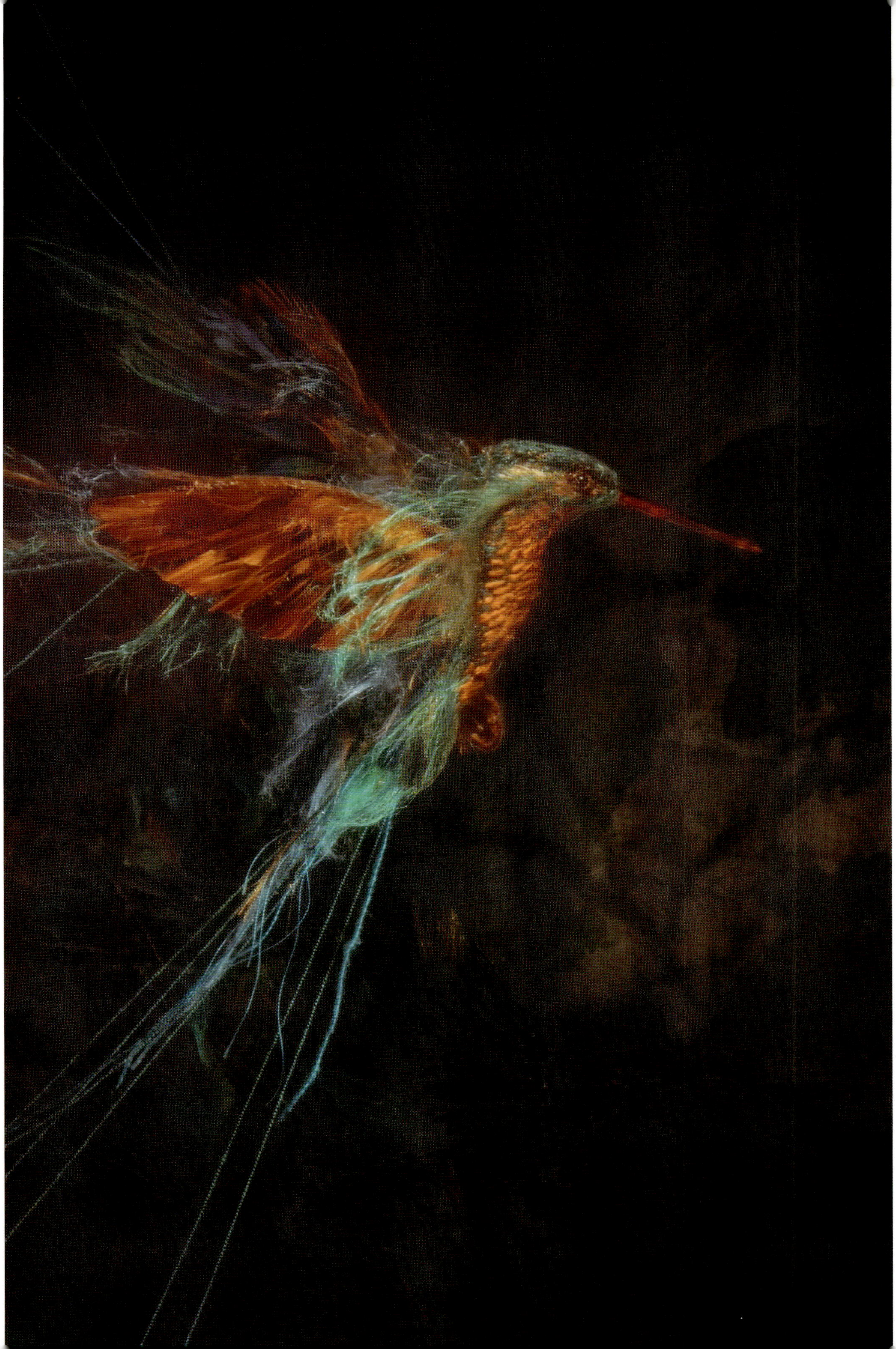

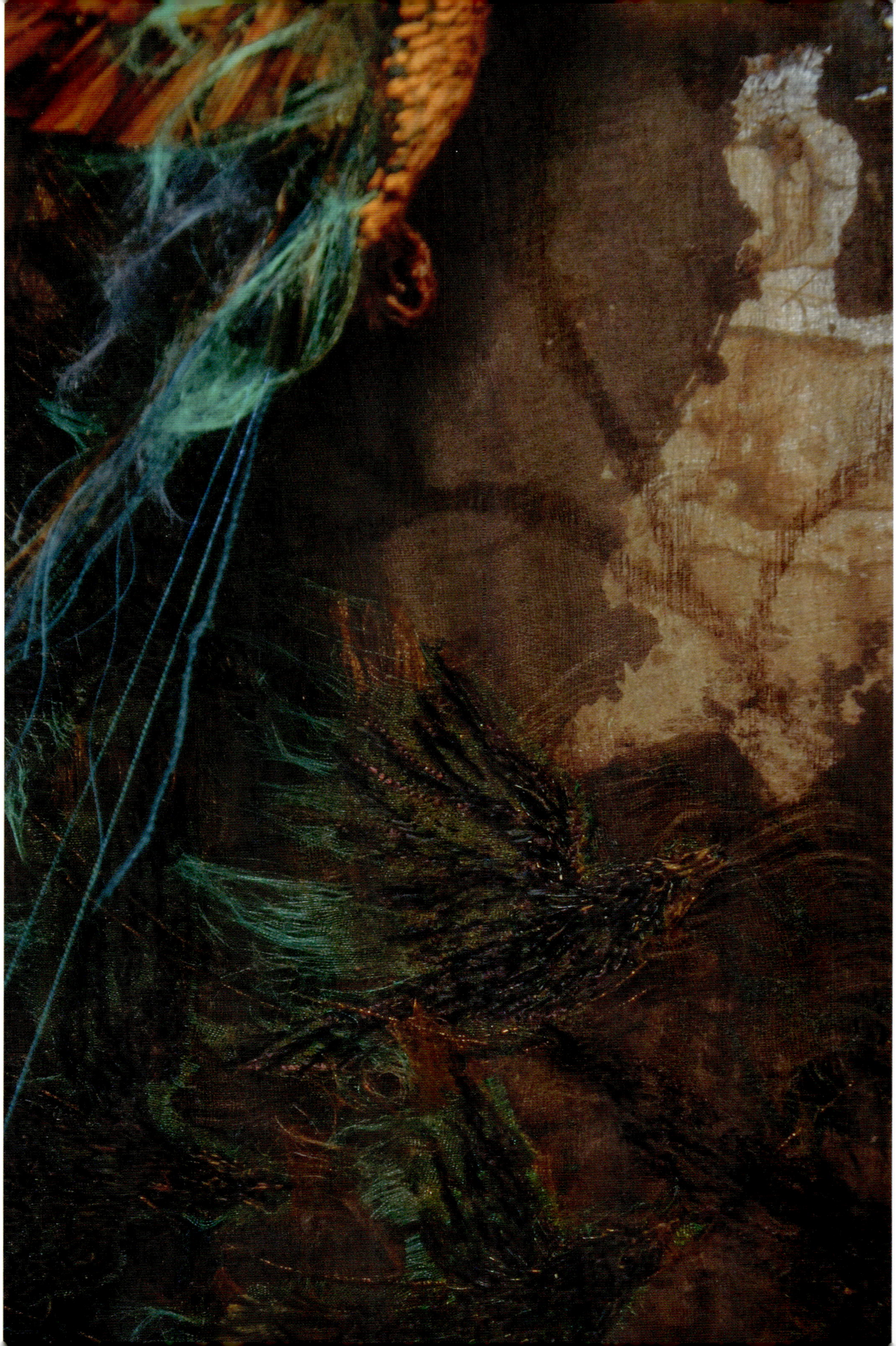

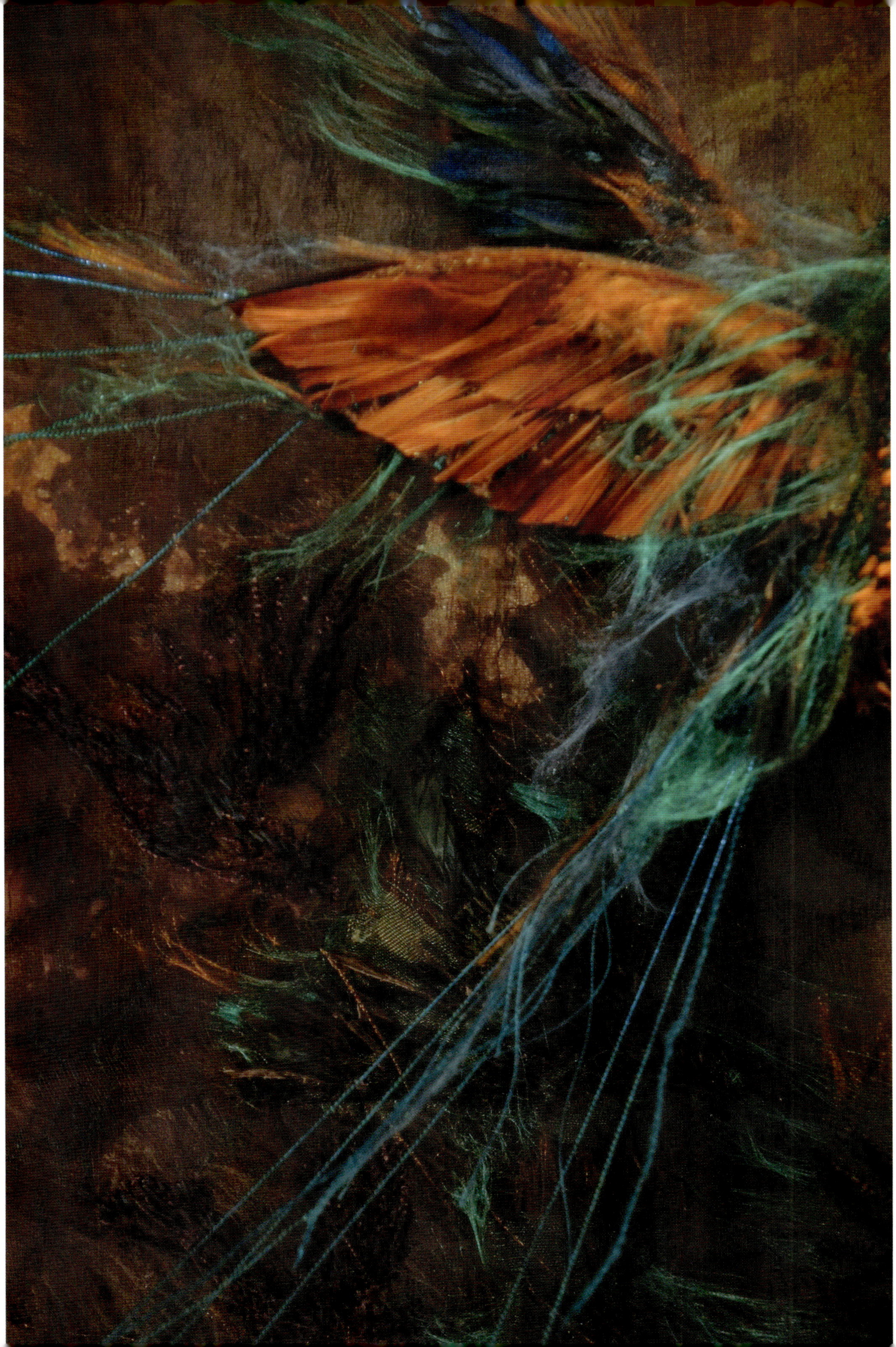

THE ARTIST'S

INSIGHT

From The Wallace Collection, Parrying Dagger
Object number: A790

The art of embroidery has been used throughout history to portray meaning through metaphor, showing place, status and tribal alignment, or to send a message. I wanted to echo this in the artworks that comprise *Trace*, with each piece taking the form of a contemporary *impresa* – an emblem laden with meaning.

The main catalyst that led me to develop my process and helped me to conceive the work for *Trace* has been my relationship with museums. Our history and heritage can be found within these institutions – they provide an understanding and appreciation of our culture and can foster a self-reflective dialogue, tracing back through our past and helping us to find meaning and context relevant to our lives and the world we live in today.

Visiting museums has been a constant in my research for both my textile conservation and costume work. Even though my medium is embroidery, I will not only look at textiles and garments, but seek inspiration from many sources: sculpture, armour, jewellery, engravings and paintings. In London, I am very fortunate to have many different museums to visit. One of my favourites is The Wallace Collection, set back from the hustle and bustle of Oxford Street, tucked away in leafy Manchester Square; it seems like a calm oasis amidst the chaos.

When you step into the entrance hall, the first painting to greet you is a favourite of mine: *The Arab Tent* by Edwin Henry Landseer. This painting, which shows a mare and her foal entwined on a rug in a tent, never fails to delight and reminds me of many happy childhood days spent with the horses at my friend's stables on the Isle of Wight. As you venture around from room to room you are treated to a fascinating array of objects and paintings, including a wonderful armoury section, as well as the interior of the building itself, which is a succession of different colour palettes and a riot for the senses.

One thing I have thought about the artefacts on display is that they are all safely guarded behind glass, illuminated and mounted as if to present their divine status and elevate their ingenuity and beauty. I can't help but feel I am in a place of worship. But as beautiful and resplendent as these objects appear, they are surrounded by empty space within these cabinets, their context spirited away by this cleansed environment they now exist in. As I look at an artefact on display, my thoughts start to fill this empty space, imagining the stories surrounding it. For me, this is particularly true of pieces of costume, which in their museum setting are like ghostly shells. I find myself imagining a character who may have owned them and the world they might have inhabited.

This process of delving into the past and searching for a character's background is part of my costume work. After research and exploration, instead of unpicking and stripping back the layers, I do the reverse by imposing and stitching a story onto the costume. As an embroiderer, I will always try to portray elements of a wearer's personality within the designs I originate, by consciously adding symbolism and meaning. Costume embroidery is not just beautiful embellishment or texture; most importantly it is a narrative tool that can express much to a viewer. So, when I study a costume, I can't help but decipher it further by looking beyond its physicality, thinking of its purpose and context, as well as what events were present within the social and political landscape of the period it came from.

When imagining the person to whom a highly decorated item may have belonged, I consider that they would most likely be someone from an affluent section of society. At this point, I start to find a duality in the piece – I question my own judgement at desiring such an item as its history unravels. I am conflicted, as I appreciate the beauty and craftsmanship, but this can be tarnished by my understanding of what the artefact may have represented: an object exclusively owned by an elite faction of society, who would mostly use it as a device to promote an image, to gain influence and power, or to express their great wealth – embodying a self-obsessed materialism, unaware or blind to the injustice and suffering of others less wealthy around them.

From the Wallace Collection, triptych miniature titled The Adoration of the Magi
Object number: S279

The dualities of these artefacts are not immediately apparent; we may need to look to the small information card, placed discreetly to the side so as not to interfere with the visual splendour of the object. This text can give us some clue or knowledge about the background of the piece, but this is not so affective; the texts don't overshadow or compete with the visual impact of the pieces on display that confront us.

It is hard to pass judgement on these artefacts with their context stripped away – we can only come to our own conclusions, which are informed by our understanding, and our awareness of the world we presently live in. Even though the object is from a different period, there is an underlying conclusion for me that can be traced, revealing that there are similarities still present today. No matter what era I look at, there are certain attributes that never seem to change within the nature of man.

Observing this void within the threshold that surrounds an artefact in a museum display, I want to explore and encroach it through my medium, bringing more meaning to the artefact. Apart from constructing a new perception, the intention was to use the works here as a process – as sketchbooks to extract ideas, techniques and themes that I can trace back into the past, but that would be relevant to the world I live in today. All this would inform the final body of work entitled *Trace*.

As I wouldn't be able to procure the ideal artefacts that I needed to inspire my work, I decided to create them myself, which would benefit my process as I could cater their designs to the desired quality and symbolism that I required to feed into the subsequent artworks. The three artefacts that would provide the inspiration, research and exploration are all costume-related to give a sense of character, context and place. They are objects of beauty, stemmed in desire; intimate pieces, creating human connections; tokens of love – perhaps given with pure intent, or they could be seen in a more negative way, as a token or bribe to gain favour, or claim ownership.

The three artefacts I have created are a late 16th century-style English embroidered gauntlet glove: *The Hand*, which inspired the artwork *All That Glitters…*; an 18th century-style French jewelled stomacher: *The Heart*, which inspired the artwork *Entropy*; and a late 19th century-style Japanese hair ornament: *The Head*, which inspired the artwork *Conscience*.

Opposite and left: at The Wallace Collection

the hand

"... You are undone if you once forget that the fruits of the earth belong to us all, and the earth itself to nobody."
Jean-Jacques Rousseau

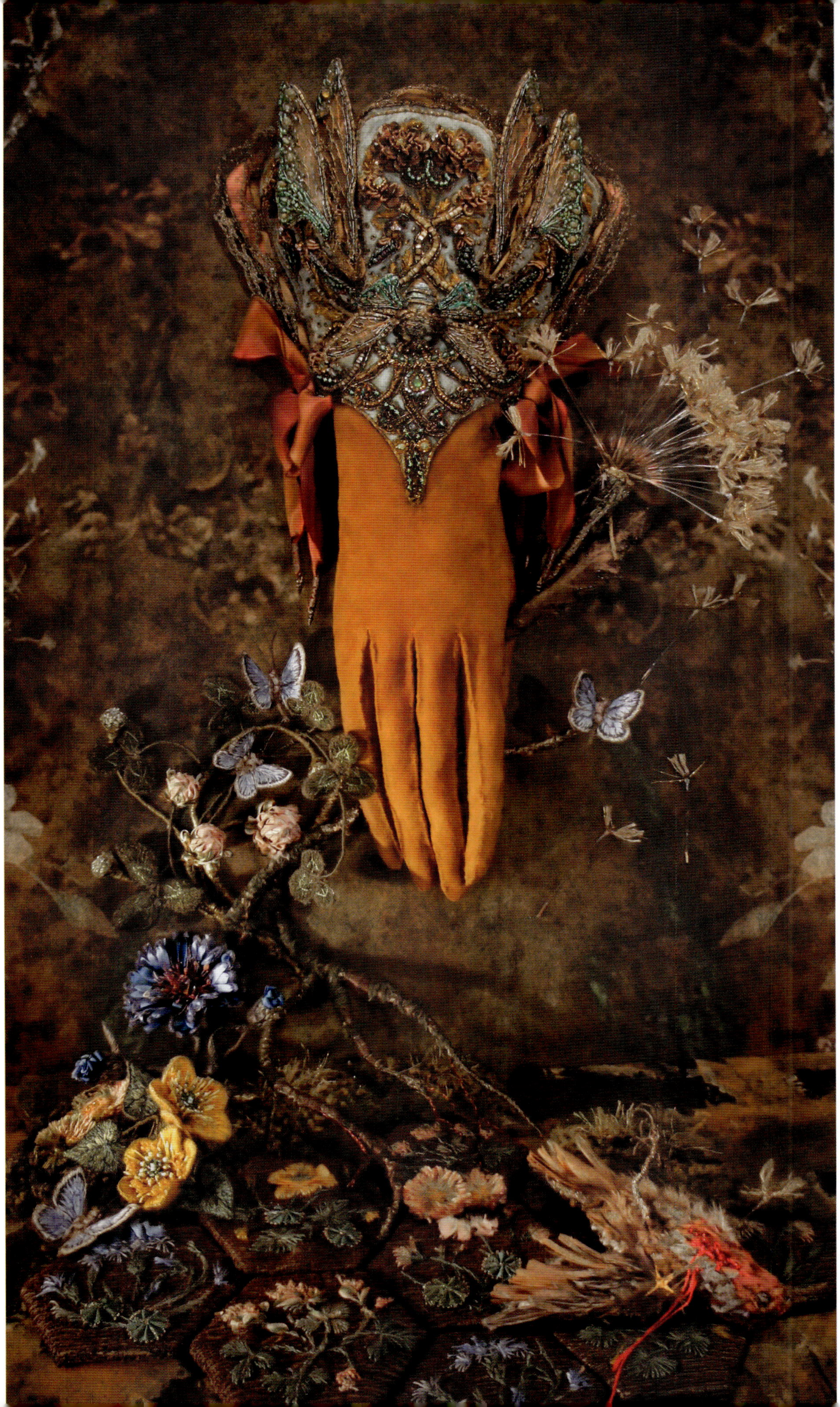

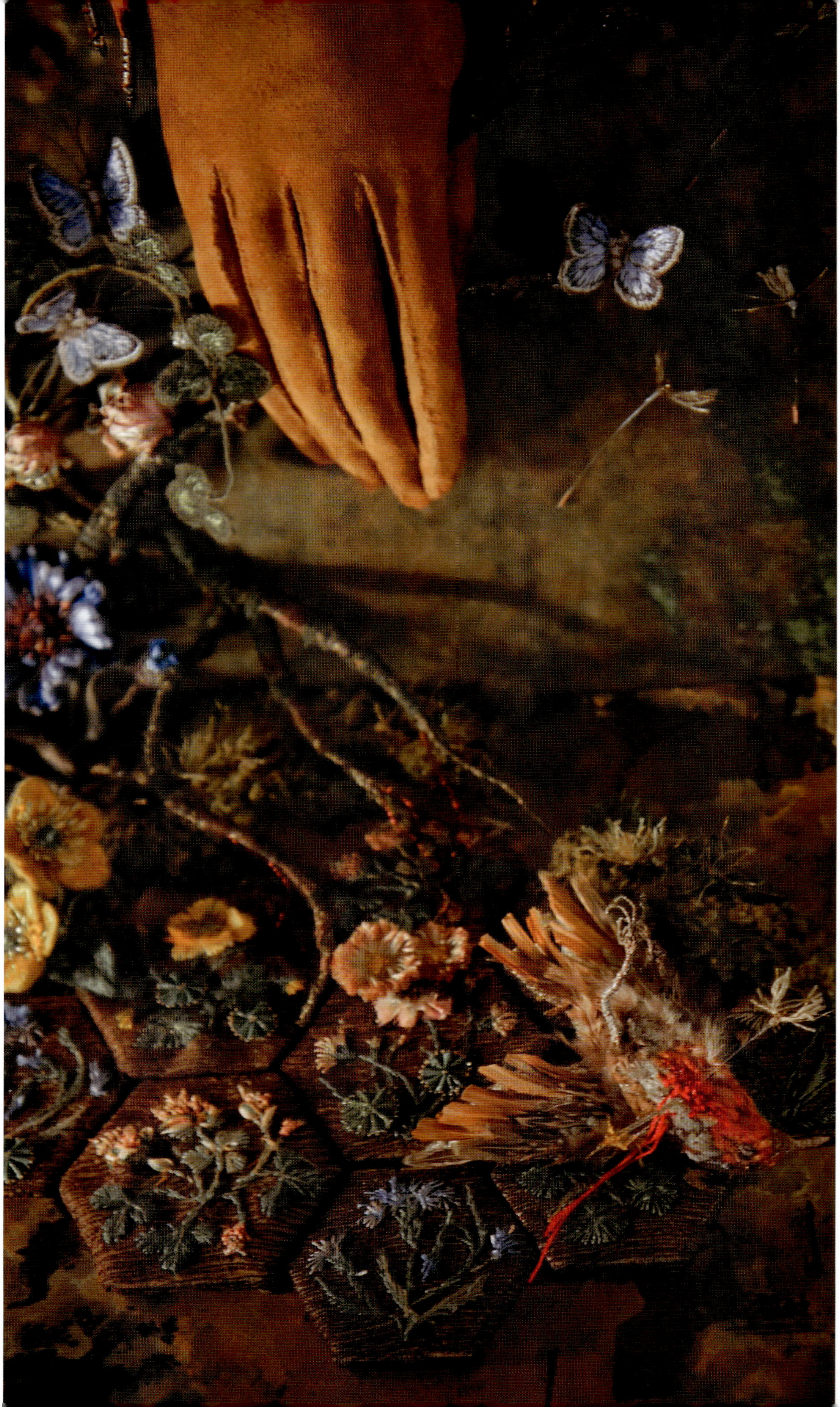

artefact insight

the hand

For my first artefact I have created a highly jewelled and embroidered glove, akin to one from the Elizabethan era (1558–1603), considered to be a 'Golden Age' during which time there was a flourishing of arts and crafts. When deciding on which artefacts to create for my process in order to develop the artworks from them for *Trace*, I found myself initially drawn to the Elizabethan era, for a variety of reasons – it is a fascinating period within our history, and when delving into the past you soon realize there are similarities echoing within the world we live in today. But most importantly, I am simply drawn to the decorative aspects of such items created in the era, appreciating the detail and skill involved in creating them, which stems from my work in costume and textile conservation.

I find the phrase 'Golden Age' to be somewhat misleading, however, as it conveys a romantic notion of a period in history. The term originates from Greek mythology, denoting a period of peace, harmony, stability and prosperity. When used in reference to Elizabethan times, it really glosses over the fact that prosperity and wealth was not available for all – it was mostly for the elite in society, never seeming to filter down to the poorest in what was a very unequal society. Peace and harmony were not that abundant either, as the ruling class lived in constant fear of losing power, due to England finding itself isolated from its European neighbours because of religious upheaval, war and trade embargoes. This lack of stability led Elizabeth I and her government to rule the kingdom with an iron fist, censoring free speech, even within the arts.

In this era there was much use of symbolism and metaphor, which allowed those with opposing ideals to speak out whilst being afforded some protection from the scrutiny and harsh consequences dealt out by the state. But the use of symbolism and metaphor were not just the pursuit of the artist or agitator. The state itself also embraced symbolism to promote its own propaganda, examples of which can be seen in the portraits of Elizabeth I, which were constructed to present the message that she was all-powerful and in total control. One such painting, *The Rainbow Portrait*, is brimming with symbolism, which I used as a reference to inspire several embroideries for HBO's 2005 production of *Elizabeth 1*. One particular piece was based on a small jewelled gauntlet that rests on Elizabeth's ruff in the painting, and to create this I used stumpwork techniques. This was the first piece of this type of embroidery that I had executed, and it initiated my passion in developing this style within my work.

Throughout my time spent in textile conservation I have had the opportunity to work on many inspirational pieces of this era. One highlight for me was a pair of gauntlet gloves, which were beautiful but strange – they are obviously not practical, not for the purpose of being worn by the owner, due to the extended fingers. These gloves were a status symbol: they were given as gifts, tokens of love, beautiful objects to gain favour, or to grasp power. Whilst stripping back the layers to preserve these pieces of splendour you cannot help but be impressed by the skills involved, and then start to wonder as to the lives of those who would have been involved in the making of such an item, uncovering many diverse stories behind each artefact.

When deciding on which artefact to choose for the Elizabethan era, because of my previous encounter I felt this gauntlet glove was a fitting choice as the focal point for the piece that I would create for my process to inspire the artwork *All That Glitters...* With the glove taking centre stage, I then set about infusing the surrounding space with symbolism and metaphor relating to the era. After many sketches and sampling ideas, I decided on a rich colour palette. I wanted to give an impression of golden dappled sunlight, lush green growth, with flowers representing wealth and industry; but there is also moss spreading over and a slight tarnishing around the edges – a little darkness creeping in.

The glove is made from tan/brown kid suede, which I chose as it has a rich, soil-like quality, binding us to the earth. To me, it shows how our hands can toil and nurture, but also destruct and destroy. I used a cicada motif alongside the flora to denote the cyclical nature of life. The dandelion seedhead can be seen as sowing seeds far and wide for the future, but there is turmoil in it being grasped and uprooted by the hand wielding power. In the foreground is a small robin, his breast pierced by an arrow. This 'Who Killed Cock Robin' imagery has been used many times through history, symbolically connected to the fall of Robert Walpole's government in 1742, and used as a means to criticize the Peterloo Massacre in 1819. For me, the robin represents a hope for new beginnings, a positive change for good that has been shot down before it can flourish and take hold.

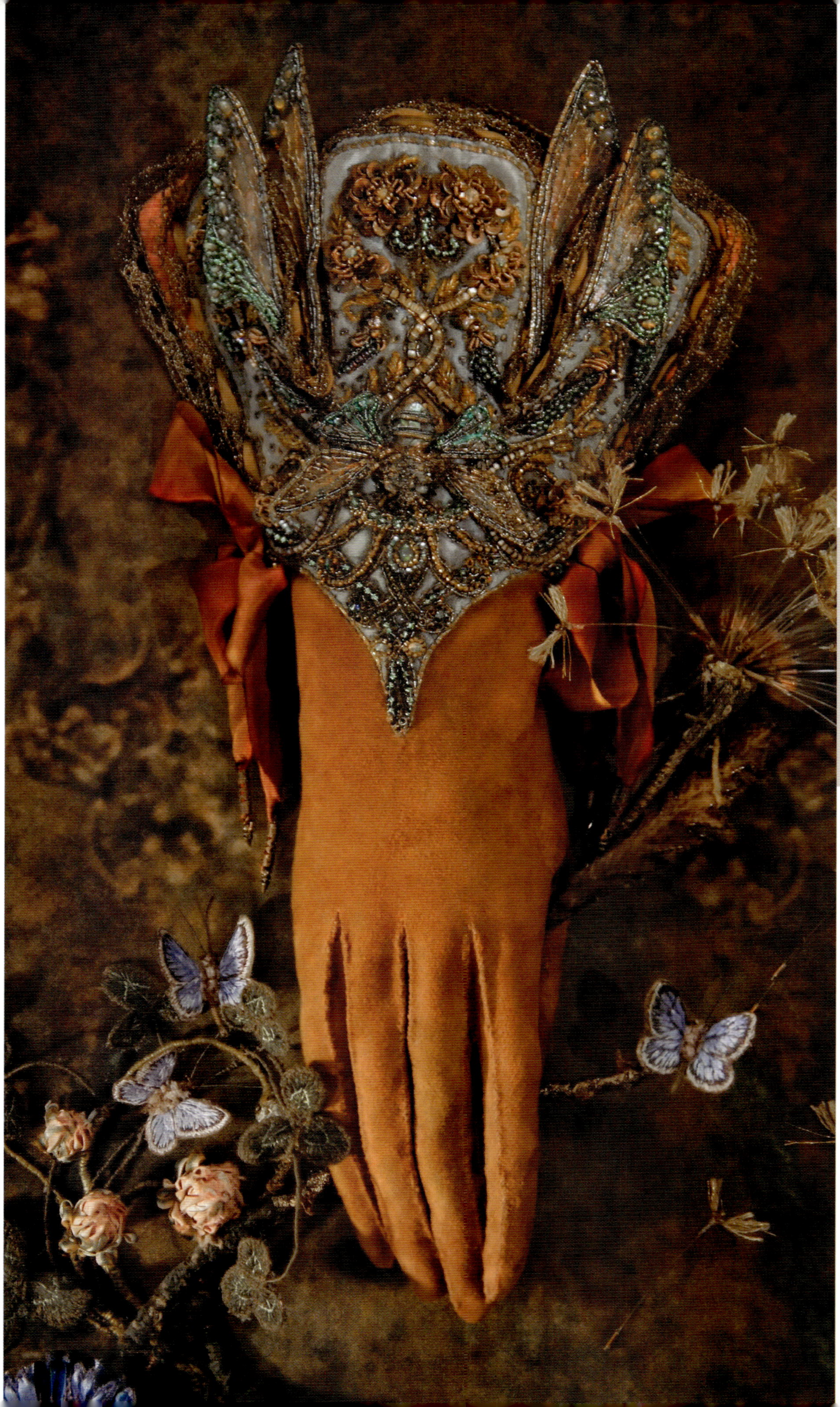

GLOVE

For the glove made in fine kid suede, I used a Janet Arnold pattern as a guide to aid me. I sketched out a design for the cuff decoration to fit the base shape, which would be made from blue taffeta. To create the jewelled filigree detail on the cuff, I embroidered this on some silk crepeline dyed to match the taffeta that would back it (see right). I often use silk crepeline as a base fabric, which is similar to regular organza, but sheerer. Although it appears to be delicate, it is quite a strong fabric and the weave doesn't open up as you stitch and bead into it. I also like it as I can dye it to match the base fabric, and it then becomes fairly invisible when laid over this. For a filigree piece like this I often, on the reverse side of the embroidery, paint along the edge with a PVA glue to hold the stitching, before cutting it out to lay onto the base fabric.

WORKING INSIGHTS

I sometimes like to use an invisible organza, rather than the silk crepeline, as it is even more sheer, but the weave is looser and therefore more unstable to work on. It also has more of a sheen but can similarly be dyed to match the garment or background fabric of the costume. Another of my favoured base fabrics is illusion tulle, but it doesn't come in many shades, mostly flesh tones, so it is not always suitable for my purpose.

As this pattern is for a glove that wouldn't be worn and is a decorative piece, the hand shape is very slim and won't fit onto the wooden articulated display shapes you can buy generally, so I needed to make an inner hand shape myself. To create this hand shape, I made the basic armature from a soft millinery wire and then wrapped this with a mesh wire to build up the shape of the fingers and hand. I then further stitched into and sculpted the shape with a green linen knitting yarn (see right).

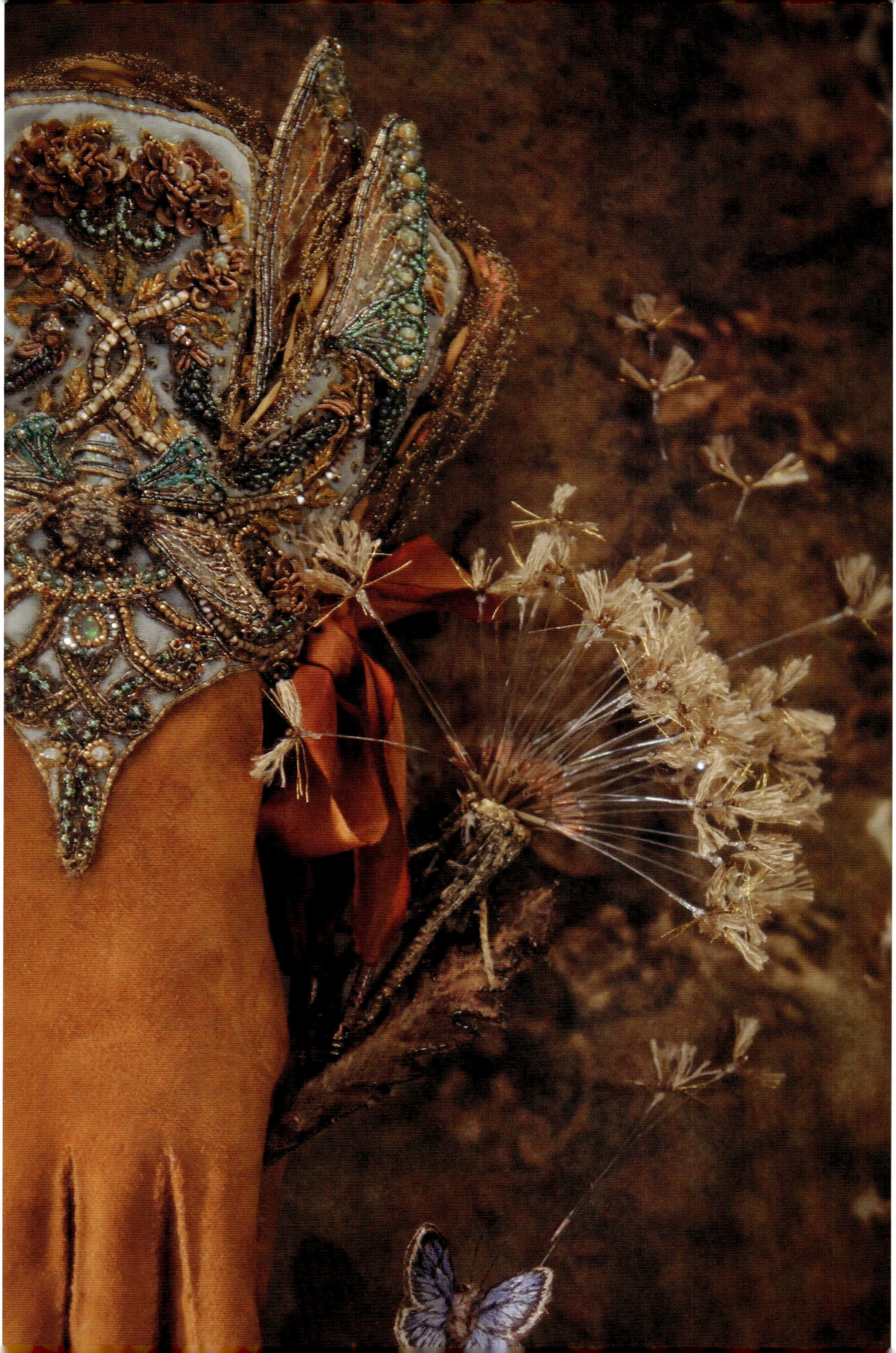

DANDELION SEEDHEAD

The gloved hand is holding a dandelion seedhead that is being uprooted, with the seeds drifting away (see opposite). The dandelion I created is a rather delicate affair, for which I used a fine fibre-optic wire, embroidery threads and French steel cut beads for the tops of each seed, with fine Indian glass bugles for the tips, all glued in place (see left). I wanted it to have a slightly tarnished, gilded feel. The fibre-optic works well visually, but as it is bent over to hold the thread and bead in place it is susceptible to breaking easily. For the purpose of a photograph it holds together, but it is definitely not a robust enough technique for a costume.

To create the seedhead base, I made a little padded dome on a piece of silk crepeline, covering the dome with silk ribbon and cotton tulle, onto which I attached the fibre-optic seeds (see below, left). Around the edge of the dome I couched mesh wire and also attached little loose tail ends, gluing the tips of these to create bracts. I made a stem from beads, threaded onto wire, encased in tubular mesh ribbon and attached this to the seedhead. The leaves are made by cutting a shape from a velvet fabric, which I glued onto a brown silk crepeline and then wired the edge before cutting the shape out and attaching it to the stem.

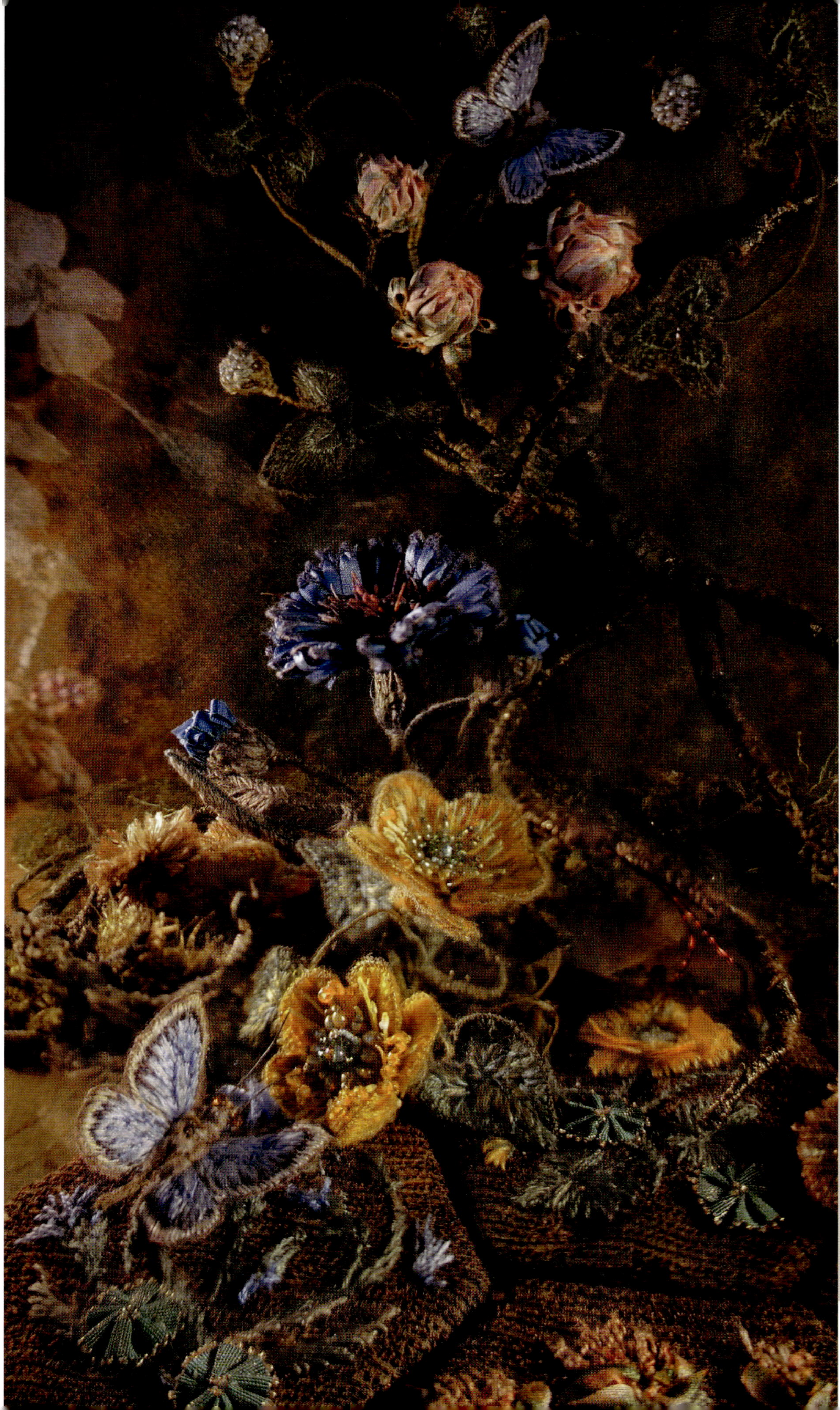

FLOWER TILES AND FLOWER GARDEN

I wanted the hexagonal tiles that adorn the base to have a suggestion of a floral decorative pattern, and to have some three-dimensional flowers growing out from this tile carpet (see opposite). These flowers, representative of industry and riches, are being drawn to the hand, and there are small blue butterflies fluttering around them.

Perspex hexagons form the base shape, which I covered with a blonde marbled silver leaf. For each tile, I stretched over a pattern embroidered on invisible organza, which I then sketched some colour detail into with fine embroidery floss. I then embroidered some three-dimensional flowers to correspond to the tile motifs. For each flower – the kingcup, the cornflower, and the clover – I needed to first break down its component parts: the petals, corolla, stamens, stem and leaves. I used illusion tulle to embroider the petals and leaves, as it gives the best finish when seen from either side, and I outlined the edges with a fine soft wire.

For the corollas I used a variety of stitch, bead and mesh wire. I made some of the stamens from thread and beads, alongside which I added some vintage ones I had previously sourced. I stitched the petals around the corolla and twisted the excess wires together to form a stem and wrapped this with embroidery thread. Once I had made the flowers, buds and leaves, I arranged all the elements together, stitching them in place and wrapping more thread around the joins.

WORKING INSIGHTS

As part of the costume embroidery work I do, I have been asked to create various corsage adornments by the designer Michele Clapton for some of her costumes, such as those I made for ballgowns worn by Nicole Kidman on the film *Queen of the Desert* (2018; see page 151). When setting out to embroider some flora, I find it helpful to look at the real thing, as well as botanical illustrations and stylized jewellery interpretations, to help me clarify the structure and components required to build each piece.

SMALL BLUE BUTTERFLIES

For butterflies, I will sometimes paint a rough guide design onto my base fabric and then stitch into this, but if I am creating multiples I will print out a design on organza to save time (see left). I will initially paint the butterfly wings on paper, create repeats to size in Photoshop® and then print this out on an inkjet organza sheet.

Once I have embroidered the butterfly wings, I press them flat and paint with a fabric stiffener; when dry, the wings hold their shape well. For tiny butterflies like these I create the bodies using a lucet cord made from two fine embroidery threads, and wrap a little chenille thread around where the body joins the wing. For their eyes I used two 2mm Swarovski faceted beads; the feelers are a fine stiffened thread (see left and below left).

WORKING INSIGHTS

In some of my costume work I have used an initial painting technique and then stitched on top, particularly when time is tight, but sometimes because it suits the desired design. When I worked on the 2005 HBO/Channel 4 TV mini-series *Elizabeth 1* with costume designer Mike O'Neill, a long draped wrap with the eyes and ears motifs on it, similar to the one in *The Rainbow Portrait*, was executed in this way. This saved me time, as the stitching didn't have to be quite so dense and the paintwork helped fill in some of the detail. Another costume on this production was made from a woven silk fabric, patterned with flowers and foliage, onto which I added beading to lift the detail and dotted tiny sequins in the surrounding background, which really lifted the design and made it look more richly embellished.

On the film *Queen of the Desert* (2018), for a ballgown that took inspiration from the designs of Charles Frederick Worth, I needed to create something to give the impression of the haute couture style of embroidery for that period. The designer, Michele Clapton, wanted the gown to have a watery and dewy feel, and another consideration for me was that it had to work for daylight and night scenes. For this I initially painted the design on the bodice and skirt panels, then embroidered and beaded into it, concentrating the embellishment on the bodice and hip areas of the skirt, trailing off and allowing the painted areas further down the skirt panels to fill in the picture. I used various beads, fish scale sequins, and tiny light-reflecting crystals that in daylight were subtle and became part of the painted design, but at night, under the film lighting, twinkled and glistened.

So whether you have the skills to paint your own design or can print out a found pattern or find something shop-bought, you can easily add an extra dimension to it with a little stitching or bead embellishment.

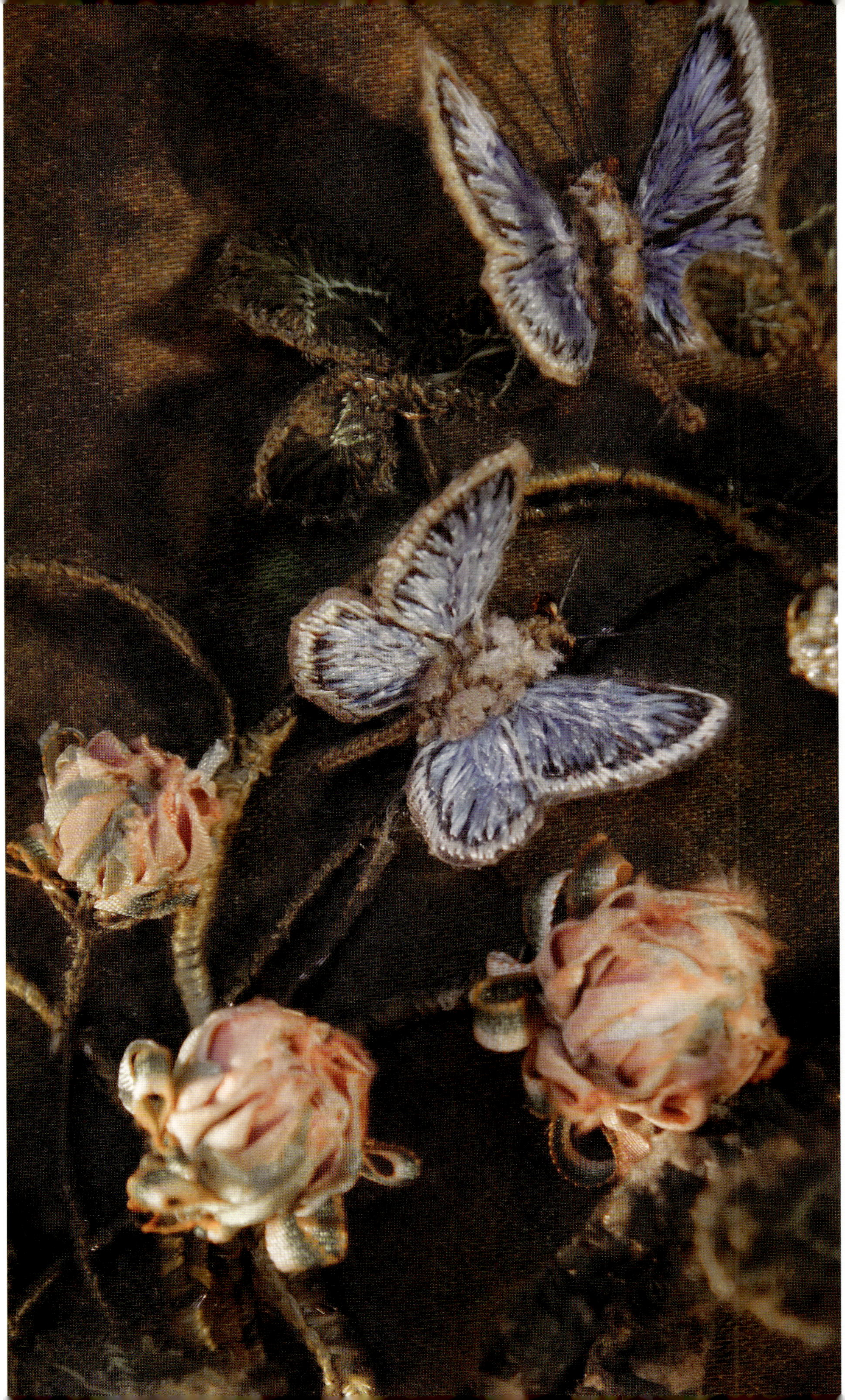

BACKGROUND FOR THE HAND TABLEAU

When I initially drew up my ideas for each artefact, I wanted there to be a continuity, imagining them all to be photographed with a dark blue midnight-sky backdrop. But as the elements came together it became apparent that each artefact would require a differing approach. Finding a backdrop is always a challenge, as you need to set the right tone for each piece. For this one I wanted a dark forest feel, where everything is lush and alive but with a tinge of foreboding. I chose to use a digital fabric print that is made up from several overlaid and digitally manipulated images of texture and embroidery – it was printed by CAT Digital at Glasgow School of Art (see opposite).

BASE FOR THE FLOOR

I wanted something that blended with the tiles and gave that dappled forest-floor feeling. I used blackened bronze marble silver leaf on Perspex and then randomly applied rust-effect paint on top – this, I felt, helped to create the mood I was after (see left).

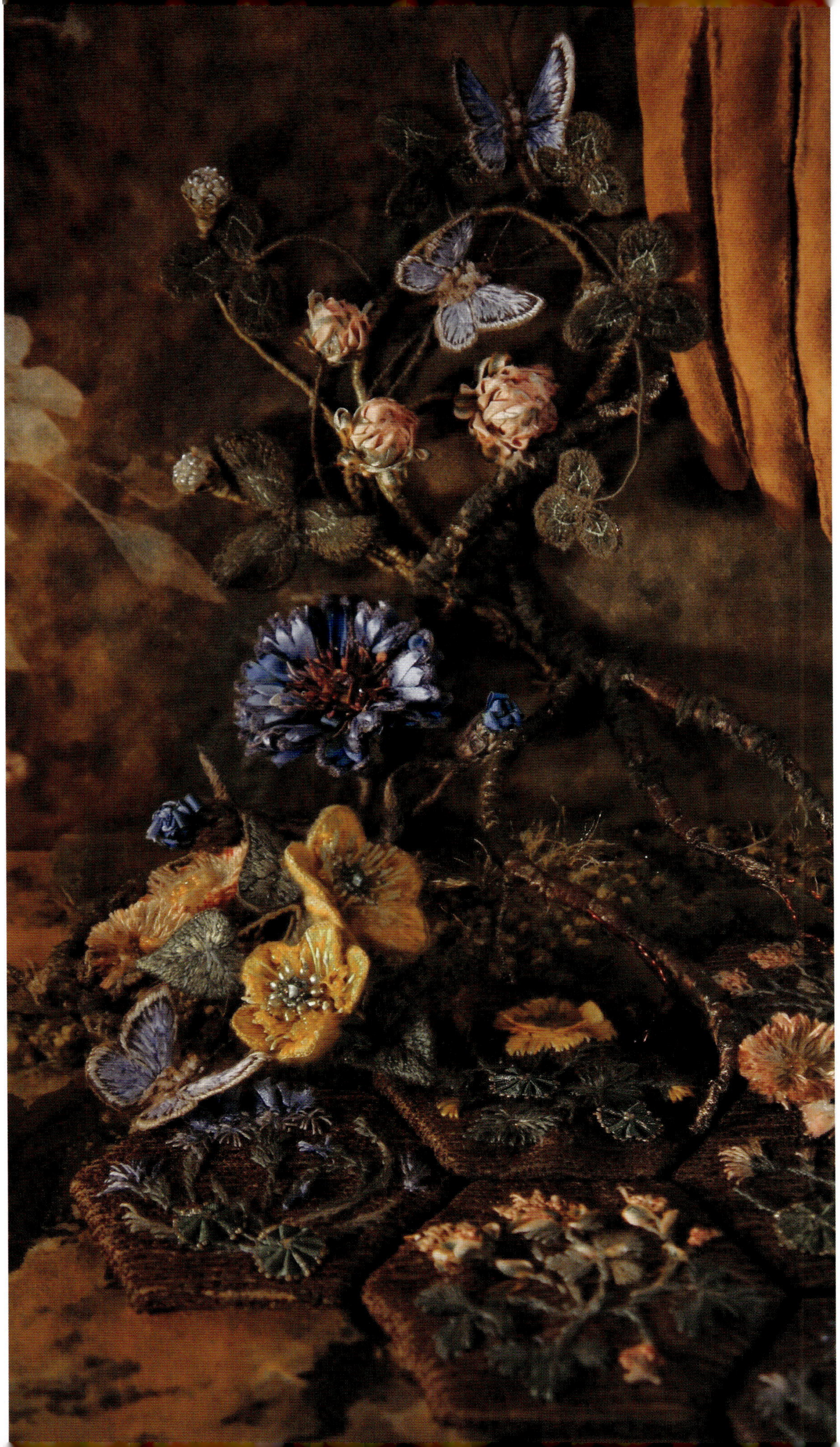

ROBIN

The small fallen robin in the foreground, nestled in the moss, his heart pierced by an arrow, is there to suggest that all is not golden in this scene. I made this bird using a needle-felting technique and added detail with various threads to sketch in the robin's plumage. I made the wings separately in a similar way; starting with a needle-felted base, I stitched in a suggestion of feather detail and then added in some real feathers to the wing edge and tail. For the wound where the dandelion-seed arrow has pierced his heart I have jewelled a small patch with Swarovski crystals and left red threads trailing – his blood flowing back into the earth.

As I worked through all these elements, my mind was moving towards the artwork that would be produced from this initial artefact. In this way, every piece I work on is instrumental in clarifying how I will approach the next. The many layers of thought are reflected in my process and execution, weaving and transcending techniques, symbolisms and themes that I explored within *The Hand*, into the subsequent artwork *All That Glitters*...

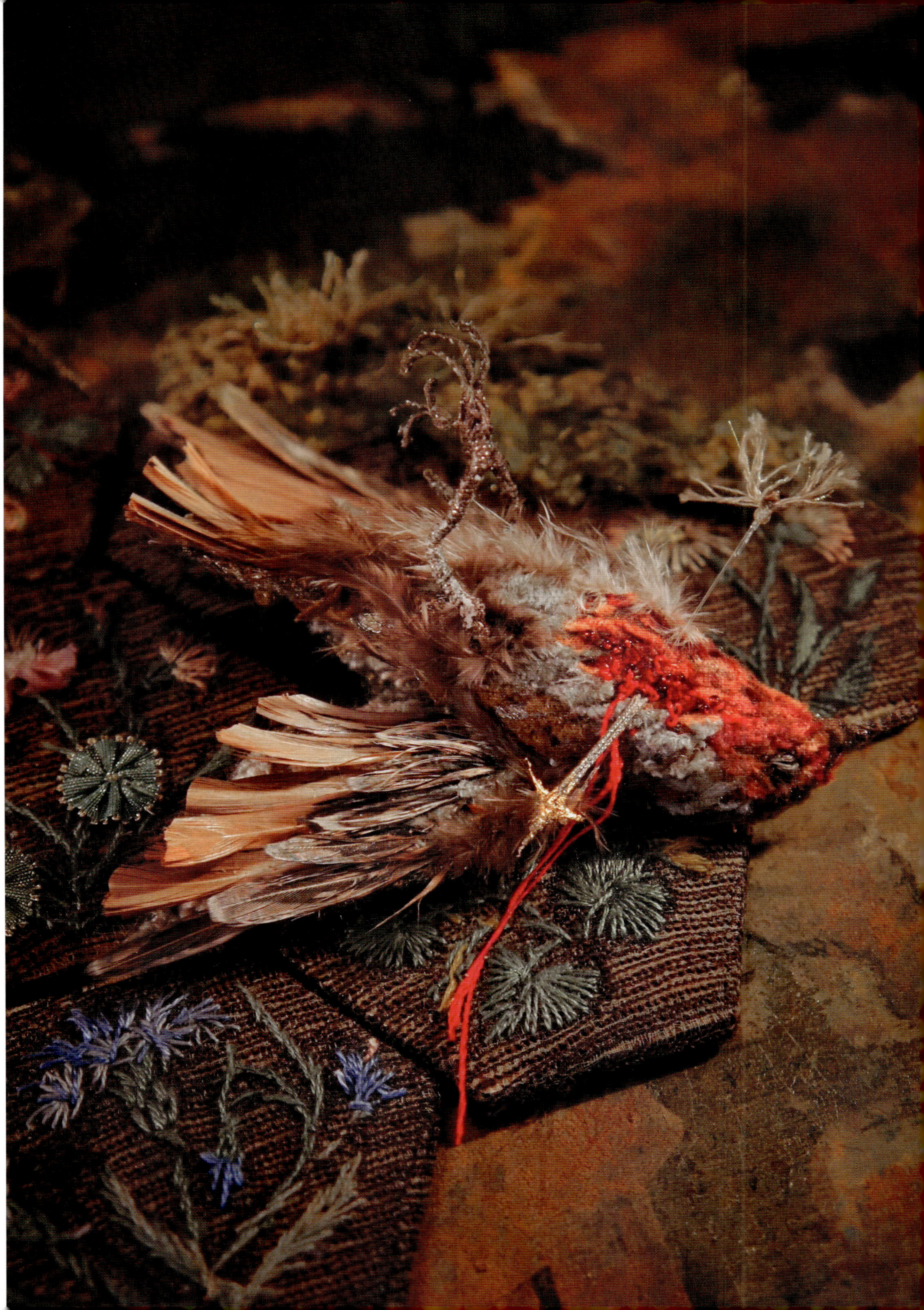

artwork insight
all that glitters...

From the artefact *The Hand*, I developed this artwork. At the centre of a dappled glade is a golden jewelled marten's head – an ostentatious display of wealth, the trace left behind of a life lived and passed from one generation to the next; a self-serving, inherited wealth.

For the background and final photography of the piece I wanted to capture the mood and feeling of dappled sunlight, similar to that which you might find in a wooded glade. To me it is reminiscent of many warm summer days spent on the Isle of Wight, my childhood home, enjoying the countryside on horseback; I recall the shelter and cooling breeze under the canopy of trees in the copse at the back of my friend's stables. The shadows and light are fleeting and constantly shifting in the breeze; as the sun fades, the light changes and the mood becomes darker. The same space I remember as a child then became more ominous, with the mind imagining danger lurking in the shadows. So although there is a predominantly golden colour and blissful warmth here, I also wanted a little rusting or tarnishing creeping in around the edges.

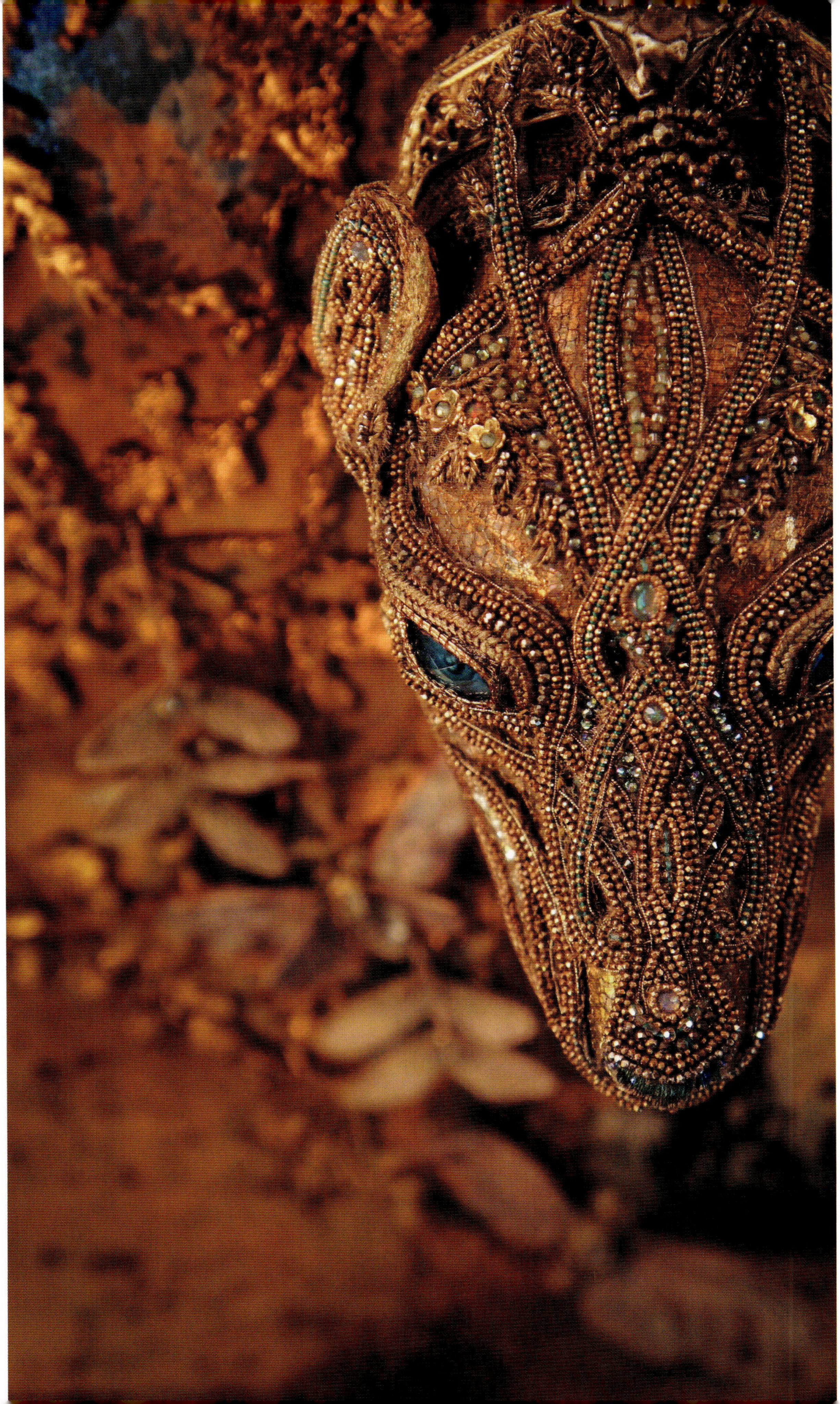

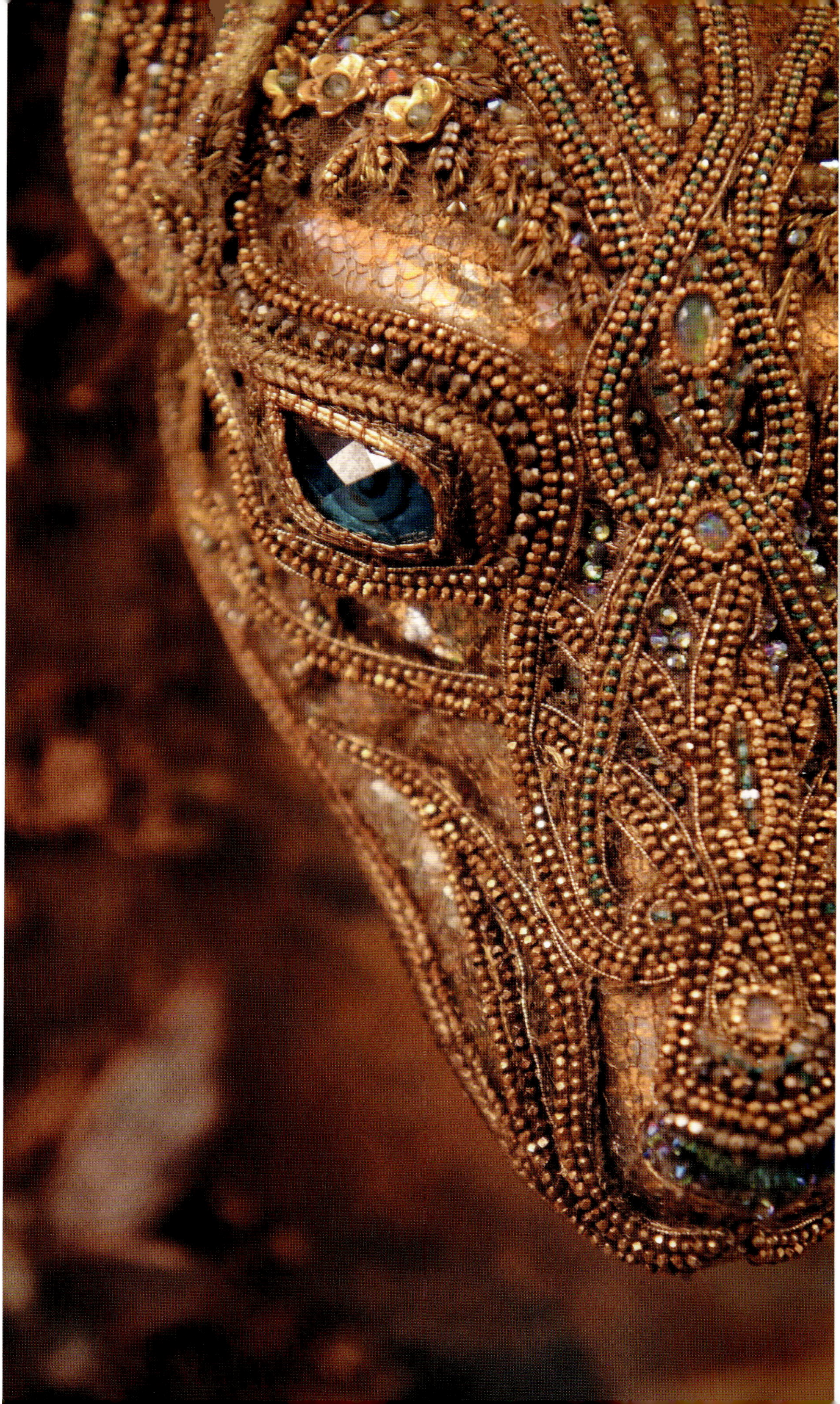

SCULPTING THE MARTEN'S HEAD

I wanted the marten's head to be a highly jewelled golden treasure. I took inspiration from the marten's head that is part of the collection at The Walters Art Museum, ca. 1550–1559, of Renaissance Umbrian origin. I began by creating the shape of the head, and I used needle felting to build up the structure.

Once I had the basic shape for the marten's head, I covered it with mesh wire and then painted it with a bronze acrylic paint mixed with fine gold mica flake. Once dry, I covered it with a layer of mesh wire and repeated this technique for the ears. I liked the hammered effect of the mica flake but wasn't sure if it was the right choice yet. I first needed to make the jewelled cage decoration that would lay over the shape to create more detail and definition before making my decision.

WORKING INSIGHTS

In my costume work I often need to create things that are slightly raised to give texture, or maybe form items that are more fully sculpted. If I just need a suggestion of relief, I will sketch out the motif, for example a bird, with thicker thread, overlay this with mesh wire and then shade into the design to bring out the detail. If I want it to be more three-dimensional, I will use needle felting, but I only do a lightly felted initial shape, so that I can sculpt it and define the features further by stitching into it.

WORKING INSIGHTS

I have often needed to emulate jewellery-type pieces in my costume work, and I have tried various approaches along the way. To achieve a more sculpted three-dimensional piece I like to make a basic needle-felted under-structure, and then create a jewelled cage to sit over the top that defines the contours of the desired shape. On HBO's *Game of Thrones* (2011–2019), I made several embroideries for the character Cersei with three-dimensional lion heads incorporated, experimenting with different threads, beads and techniques. In season 3, I created some stumpwork lion heads with a filigree backdrop for one of her more informal-style dresses, a rust red kimono (see page 153). Then in season 7, I was asked to create something reminiscent of jewelled armour, consisting of a gorget (throat covering) and pauldrons (shoulder armour). The Chief Cutter on the show, Carole O'Neal, created the shapes of these pieces for me to work on; the base shapes were made in the workroom and covered in the fabric of the dress. I then made filigree sections, some stumpwork lion heads for the side of the shoulders and a small one for the front of the neck, adding much cording and beading as well as some glass spikes. I think this was one of my favourite pieces to work on (see pages 158–159).

For the final season of the series, the costume designer Michele Clapton showed me her illustrated designs for the character Sansa Stark's coronation outfit – she had drawn a direwolf head decoration as part of the draped stole/collar (see page 173) and imagined this to be embroidered somehow. So I set about creating a version of the historical marten's head but with the direwolf shape as the sculpted motif, as this was the Stark family's house sigil.

On each project you learn new techniques and find new materials, always experimenting and evolving ideas. For this one I had bought some smoky quartz faceted slices thinking they may suit as eyes if they were drilled from the back and had other stones set in from behind as the pupil and iris. I was introduced to Emma Barnes who practises lapidary (gemstone cutting), as I didn't think this was something I could manage myself with a clamp and a drill! I described what I was after and waited to see what she would come up with… and the results were amazing. Emma had drilled into the back of the quartz, creating the space to set a small faceted black diamond bead as the pupil surrounded by a yellow glue, which from the front, because of the depth of the slices, was quite subtle. I backed these onto a silver leather to set off the iris and give depth to the eyes.

My first sample for this piece had a needle-felted base shape covered with dark mother-of-pearl veneer encased in black mesh wire. I set the eyes in place and created the filigree cage shape to sit over the direwolf head, giving more detail and contouring, which worked quite well. In the final version for the costume we used just the cage shape to give a suggestion of the direwolf head, as the complete jewelled head was too overpowering and distracting.

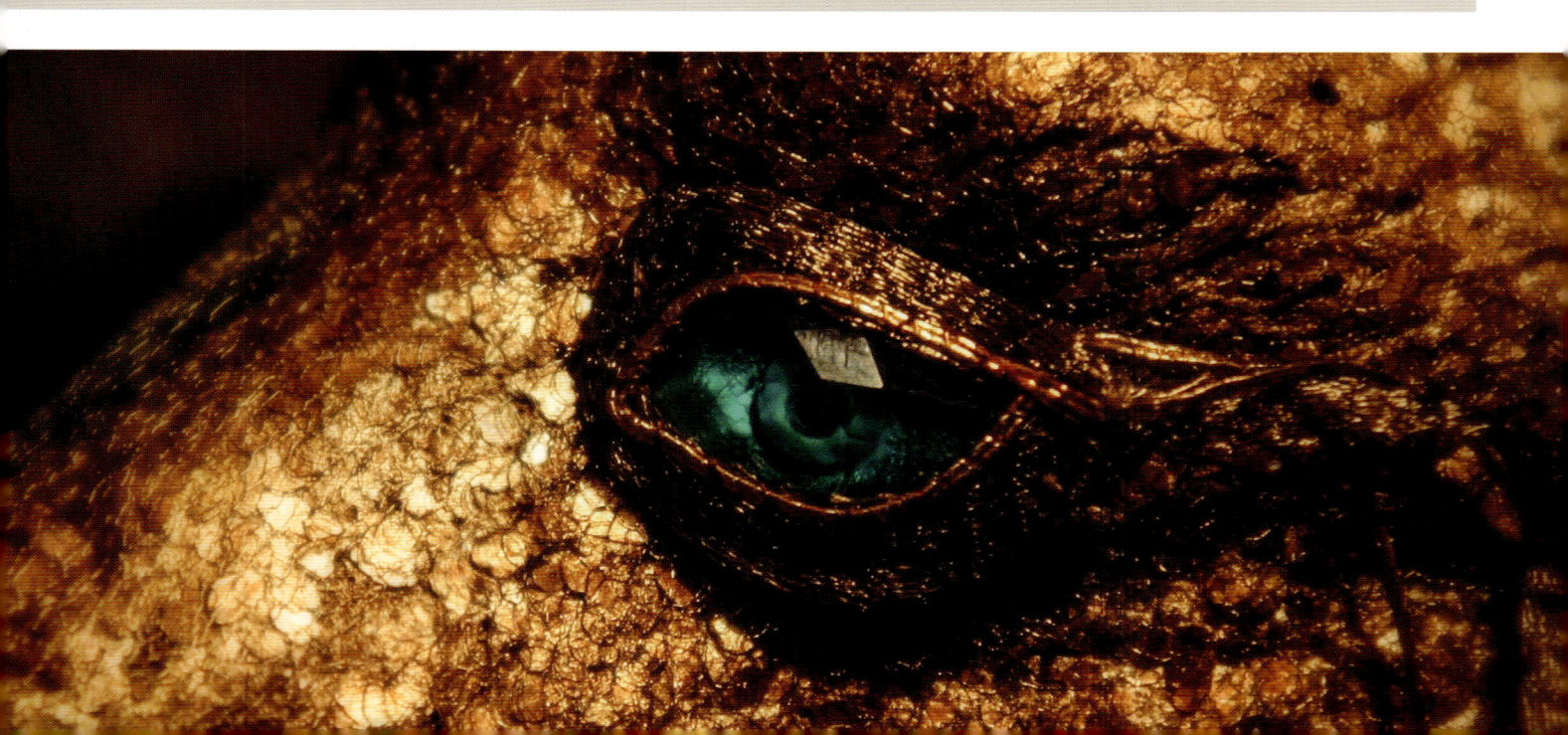

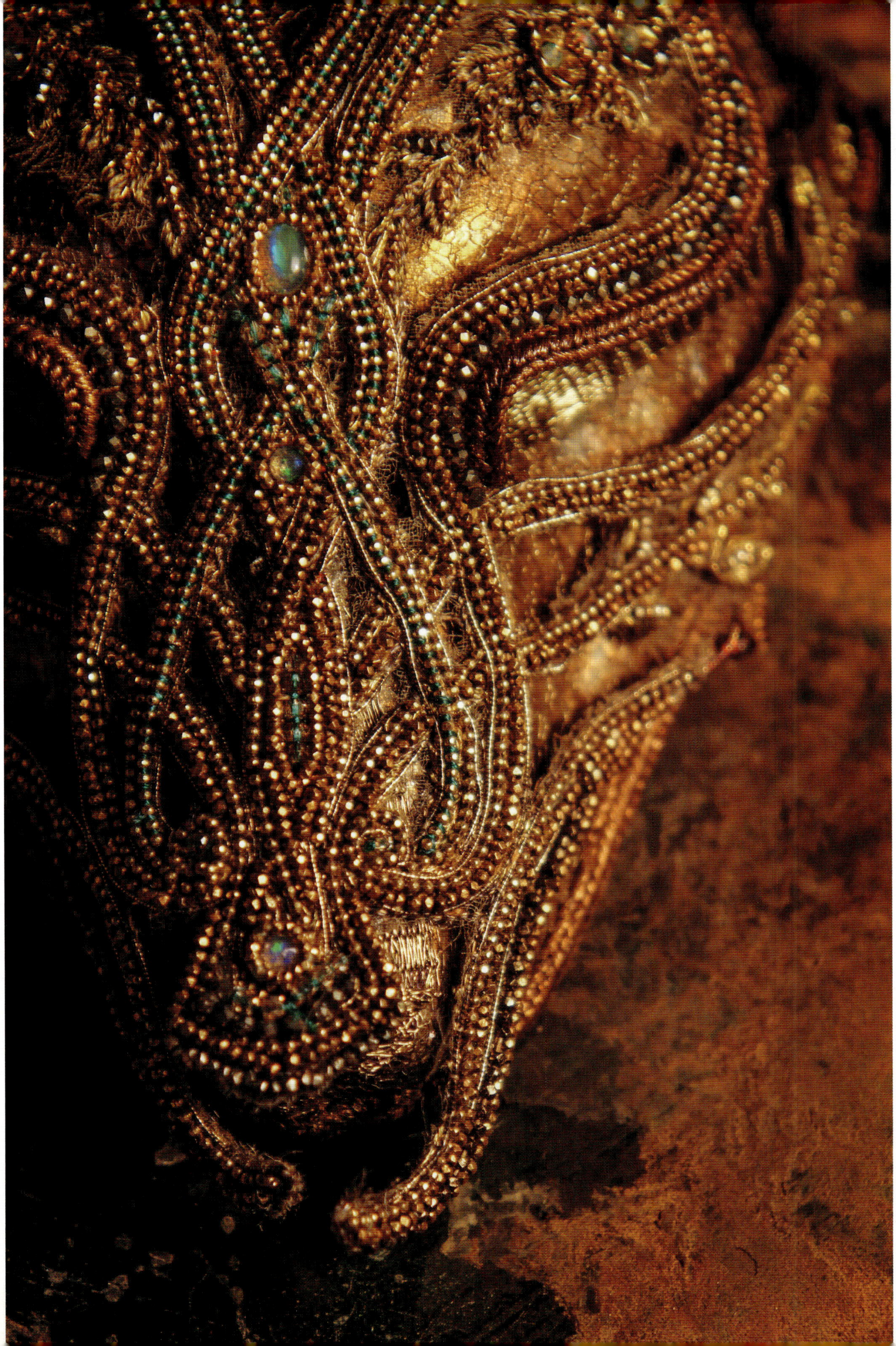

For my golden marten's head I had in mind that I wanted some blue eyes cut from a suitable gemstone. I contacted Emma Barnes again, and this time she cut faceted slices from a synthetic London blue topaz. She then drilled into the backs, setting small black nail heads as pupils with vintage mother-of-pearl flat buttons behind these as the irises. I laid these onto a silver leather to allow the irises to 'pop out' a little.

I created a gold filigree cage, marking out the design on silk crepeline, initially laying a gold mesh wire down as the base shape, outlining this with a gold Japan thread and a gold faceted ball chain. I jewelled sections with Ethiopian opals, which I love as they have a wonderful green flash to them. I have been fascinated by opals from a young age, as my mum had a ring with an opal at the centre and I loved how it looked. Opals to me seem as if they have the essence of life captured within.

Once this cage embroidery was finished, I painted PVA glue on the back to hold the edge stitches, before cutting it out of the silk crepeline. Now I could place it over the sculpted head and look at how the layers were working. I decided to cover the base shape with a mother-of-pearl veneer that I had worked a little Goldfinger paint into. To do this, I cut a basic shape out of the veneer that I snipped darts into to help it wrap over the base – but this didn't cover in one piece, so I had to add small inserts to complete the coverage. I stretched a gold mesh wire over the shape and pulled it tight so the mesh is barely there visually; this looked much more like what I had in mind. I also created small decorative filigrees for the ears, which I could pin in place.

For the collar (see opposite), I used some leather wrapped with a vintage trim and a metal filigree strip. Trailing out from this collar I have used some water chestnut beads strung up as a suggestion of a bony spine – all that is left behind of the body.

85

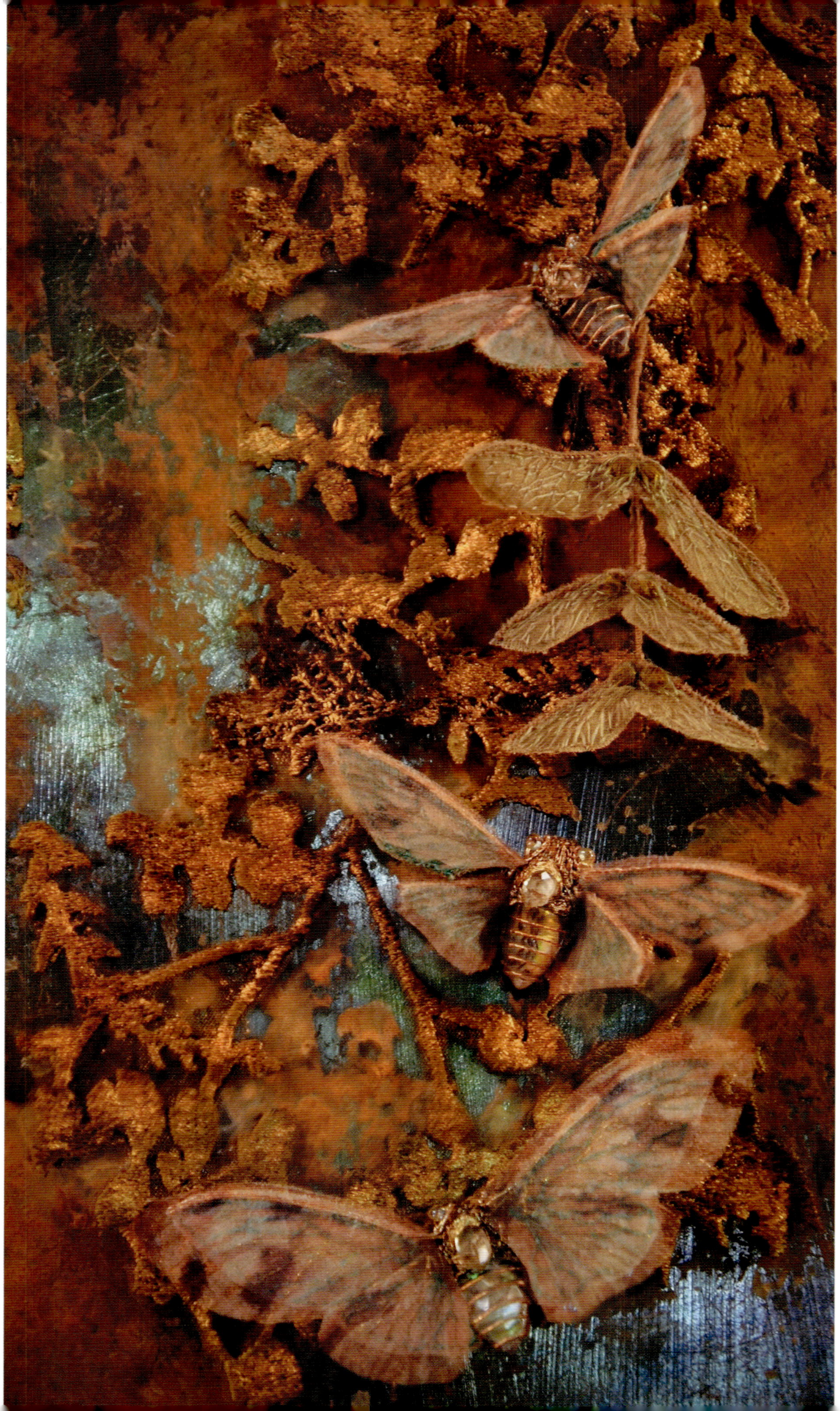

CICADAS

I have always loved insects for their jewel-like qualities and barely-there iridescent wings; as a child I would collect any dead butterflies or bees that I found when out in the countryside and keep them in boxes at home to look at from time to time. For my A-level art qualification I painted one piece that was of the metamorphosis of a moth from its chrysalis to winged beast, and for another piece I incorporated some bees and honeycomb into a textile design.

WORKING INSIGHTS

My first chance to embroider insects onto costumes was on HBO's 2005 TV mini-series *Elizabeth 1*, which starred Dame Helen Mirren. It was for one of her informal robes, which took inspiration from the bodice decoration present in a portrait of Elizabeth called *The Rainbow Portrait*. As it was a small costume team, I was sourcing and buying fabrics as well as creating some of the decorative work. For this piece I started by using an upholstery taffeta that had some subtle plants embroidered onto it – this was my base to which I could add some hand embroidery to get the desired look.

When I started on this production I came across the books of Jane Nicholas, who has been a master of stumpwork embroidery for many years and has written a variety of wonderful books. I found her *Stumpwork, Goldwork and Surface Embroidery Beetle Collection* (2004) particularly useful to aid me – I even embroidered one of her little chartreuse longhorn beetles onto this costume as an homage. Her books also helped me when setting out to create the insects for the Qarths on *Game of Thrones* in season 2; the books were insightful for me as to how to go about creating the separate elements required to then construct my own creatures. I experimented with many different threads and beads; I am never trying to create a replica of nature, merely capture some of the essence of it in what I am working on. So, finding the right materials and colour palette are essential for me, and I may go through several stages of layering stitch, bead, ribbon and paint to get to my desired end result. Each piece will develop as I work on it and allow it to evolve; I adapt my approach to suit, as the piece dictates.

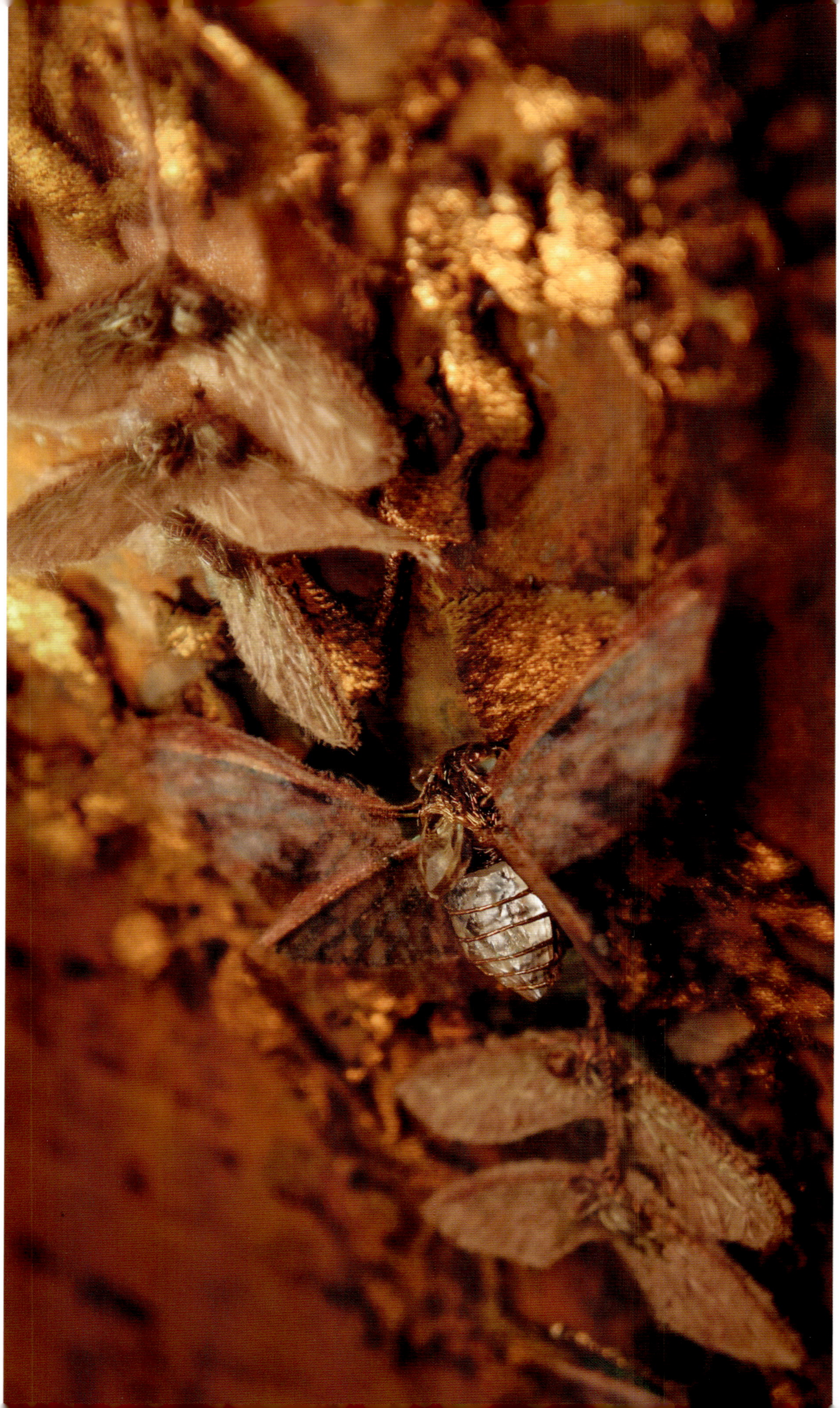

I wanted to use cicadas in this piece because as well as being a sign of summer and a symbol of rebirth and longevity, they also prune the weak branches of trees, getting rid of the dead wood. The tree benefits by not wasting its energy on a weak or diseased branch.

I love the colours of the emerging cicada and used them as my starting point. Again, I contacted Emma Barnes for her lapidary services as I wanted the abdomens to be cut from some kind of gemstone. I settled on a green amethyst, which she cut to the shape I wanted, faceted the top and etched grooves across this, into which I laid a gold Japan thread. I backed the amethyst abdomens with abalone veneer and stitched them onto a silk crepeline base. Using a sorbello knot stitch and mesh wire as my thread, I created the head and body base. I came across this stitch in a publication by Jan Beaney and Jean Littlejohn, who have written many fantastic books on a variety of stitches, some like this one that you don't find referenced in most stitch bibles. I then wrapped the sorbello stitch with more mesh wire and stitched into it with a fine metallic thread. I added another gemstone on the abdomen – this time a lemon faceted quartz marquise backed with abalone veneer – and for the eyes I used Miyuki drops.

For the wings, I wanted to create a suggestion of movement by using layers. I created the basic shape by printing out a muted butterfly image on organza, laying another piece of organza over it and stitching out the vein lines of the wing. Along the top edge I attached a green wire using buttonhole stitch, adding a vintage gold passing thread over the top of this. After cutting the wing out, I lightly glued another printed wing overlaid at the top edge – this softened the veins and gave the illusion of movement I wanted. Using a chenille needle, I threaded the wires of the wings through the cicada body, using a crimp bead on the back to secure them, trimming back the excess and stitching the wires down to the underside. After cutting the cicada out of the organza base, I tucked back the excess and stitched it to the underside.

For these I decided against legs, as I thought it may look too heavy and creepy, whereas I wanted something more magical and fairy or firefly-like for the mood.

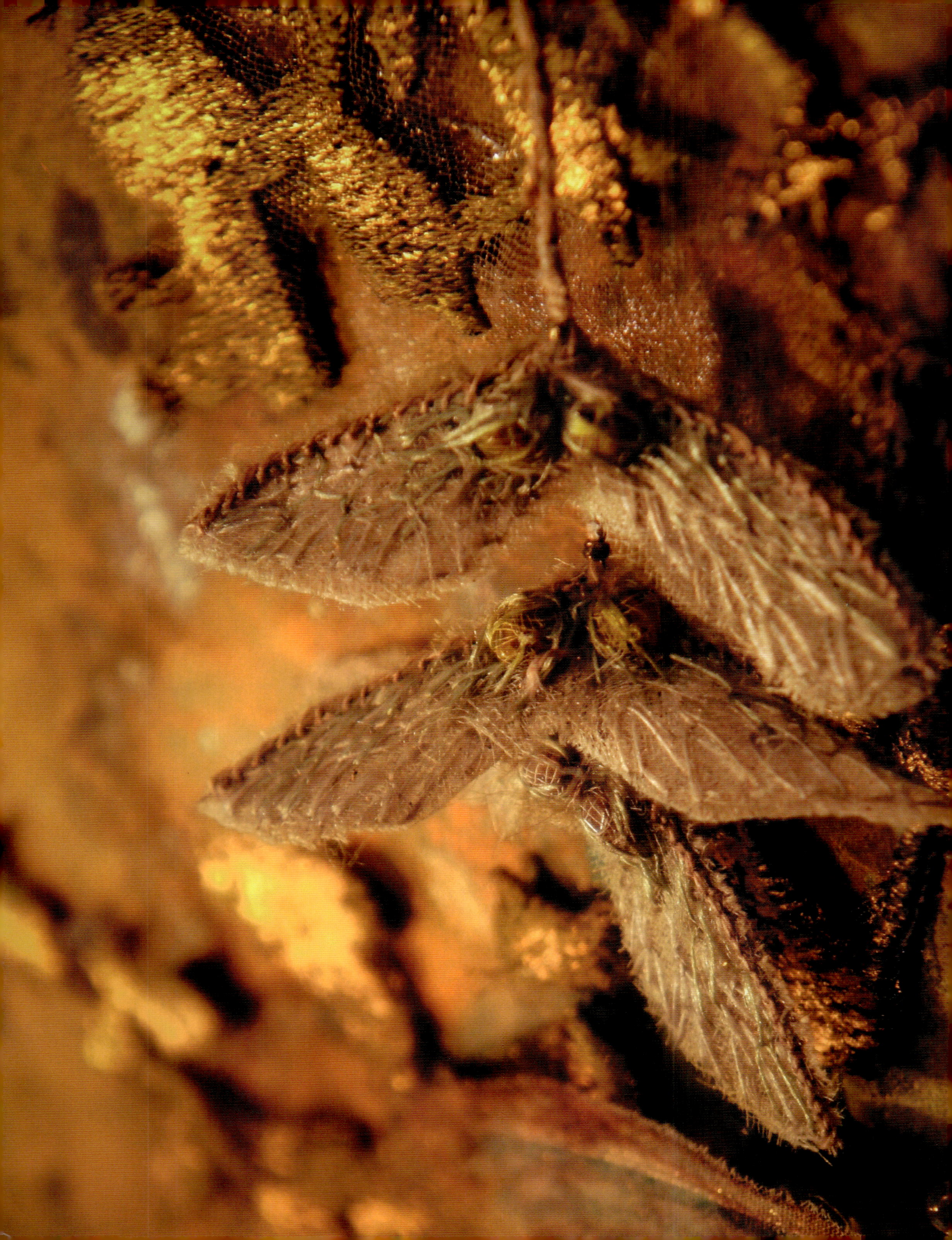

SYCAMORE SEEDS

In amongst the cutwork foliage I have added some sycamore seeds, as these trees are known for spreading far and wide, colonizing all kinds of habitat. In some scenarios they are a success story, in others an invasive species.

To create my sycamore seeds, I started by sourcing suitable fabrics for them. I laid a piece of fine vintage wool twill fabric over an organza and stitched out a rough guide outline for the helicopter seed shape. I then stitched random veins into this outline shape using fine silk floss thread, adding a Czech glass bead on each side and laying an invisible organza patch over each, further stitching into this with the silk floss. I couched down a bronze colour wire across the top using buttonhole stitch, passing the ends of the wires through a tiny French steel cut bead and then wrapped the thread ends around the excess wires to create their stems, gluing to fix (see top left). I cut the seed shapes out from the fabric base and glued the raw edge with a clear-drying PVA (see below left). I then arranged these seeds onto the background, drifting down from the cutwork foliage.

Once the background was complete, with the sycamore seeds hanging down gently from the trees, I arranged the cicadas around the central marten's head, where they have pruned back the dead wood, creating a clearing for the focal point.

the heart

"It is in one's heart that the life of nature's spectacle exists; to see it, one must feel it."
Jean-Jacques Rousseau

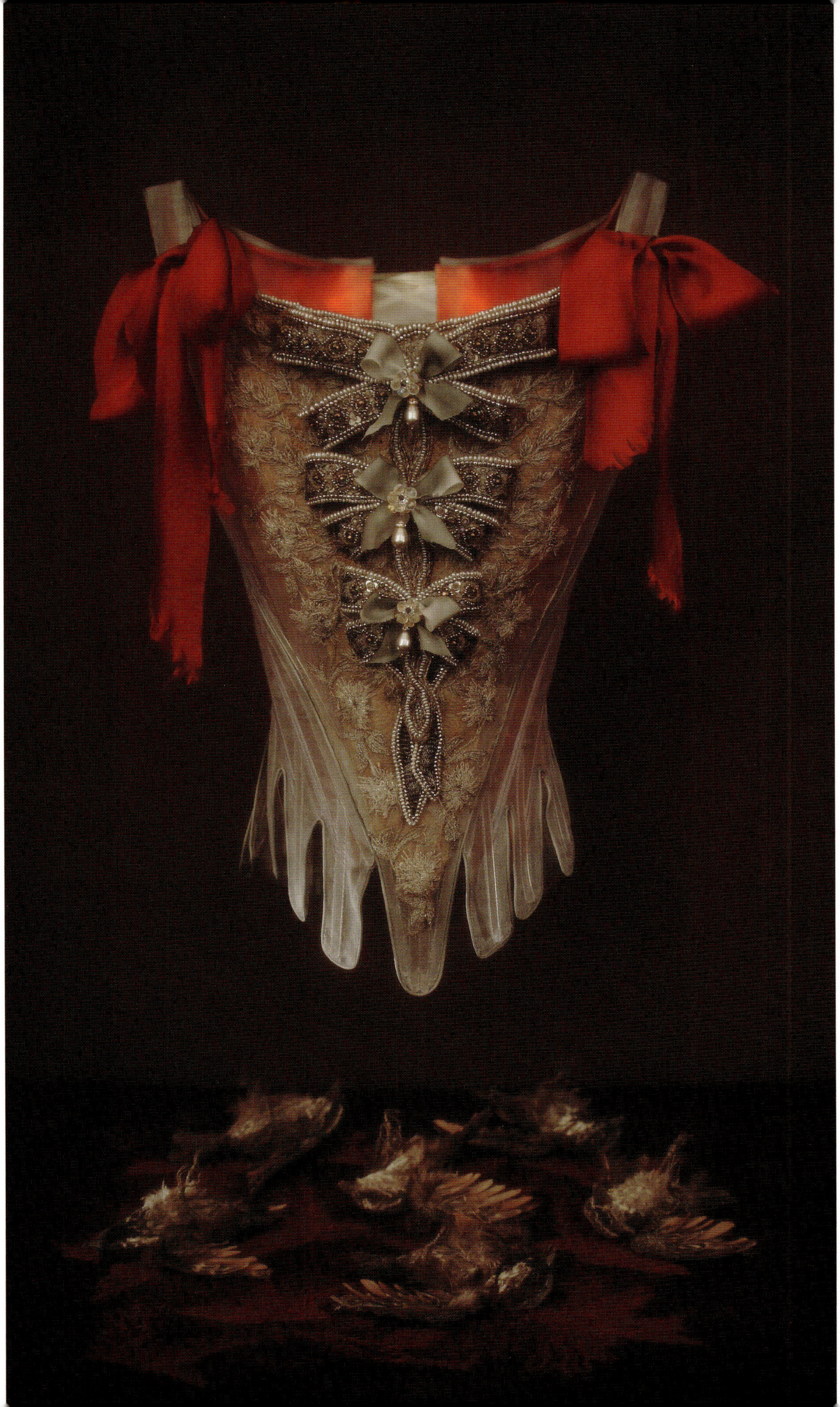

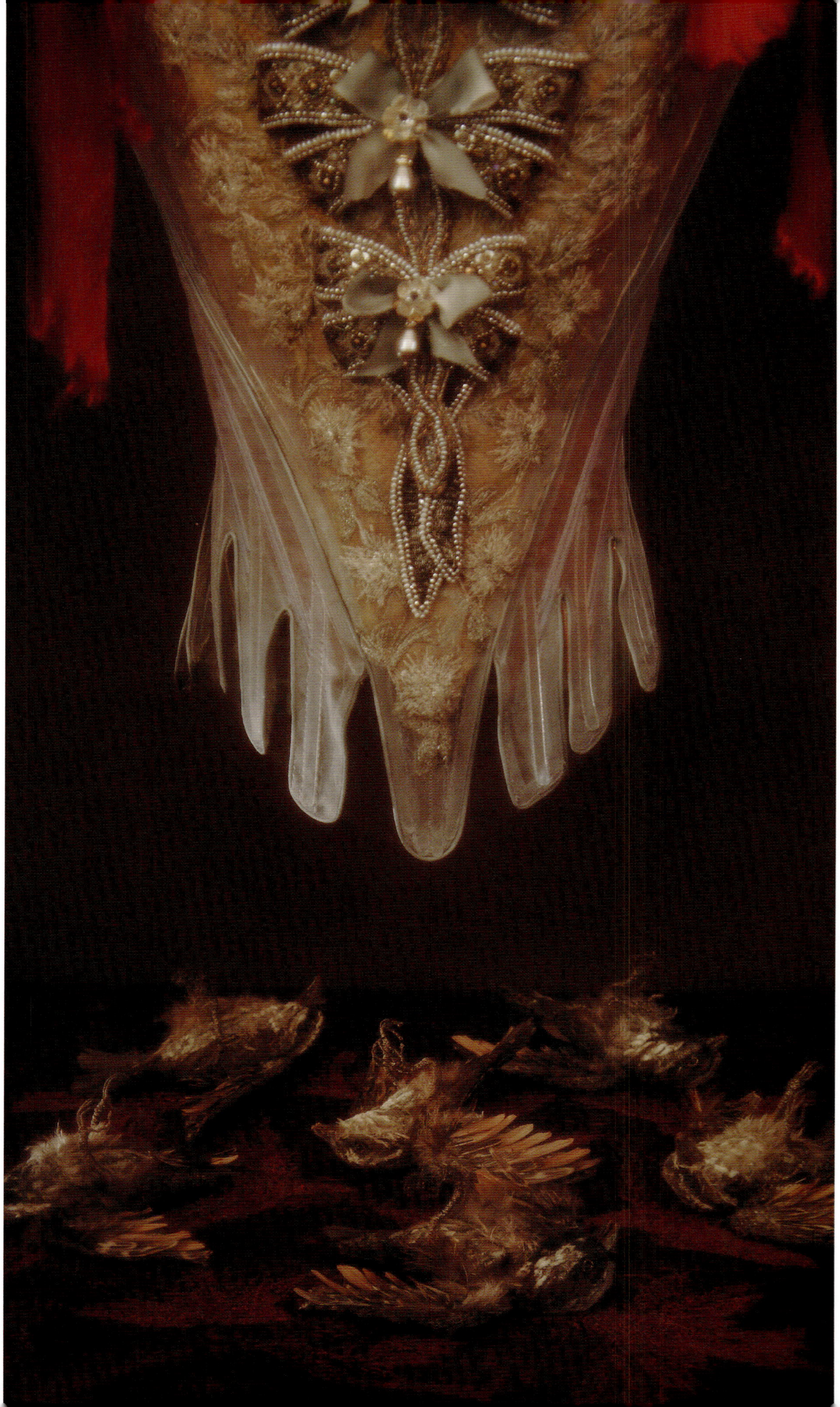

artefact insight

the heart

My second artefact, an 18th-century jewelled stomacher, sits at the front of a barely-there, vacuous corset. The bodice could be seen as holding the heart close, protected – a lover's gift binding one to another, or as a barrier to shield the wearer from having empathy for those deemed not to be in their circle. The style and decoration shows great wealth and in its setting suggests the decadent 18th-century French court. This era is well-documented for its excess and blind disregard for poorer citizens, something that is repeated throughout history around the world. The corset and stomacher are hanging in the air, below a dark blood-red ground with shadow sparrow patterns stitched into it in red. Laying on this blood-soaked carpet are six dead sparrows; the scene evocative of the French Revolution.

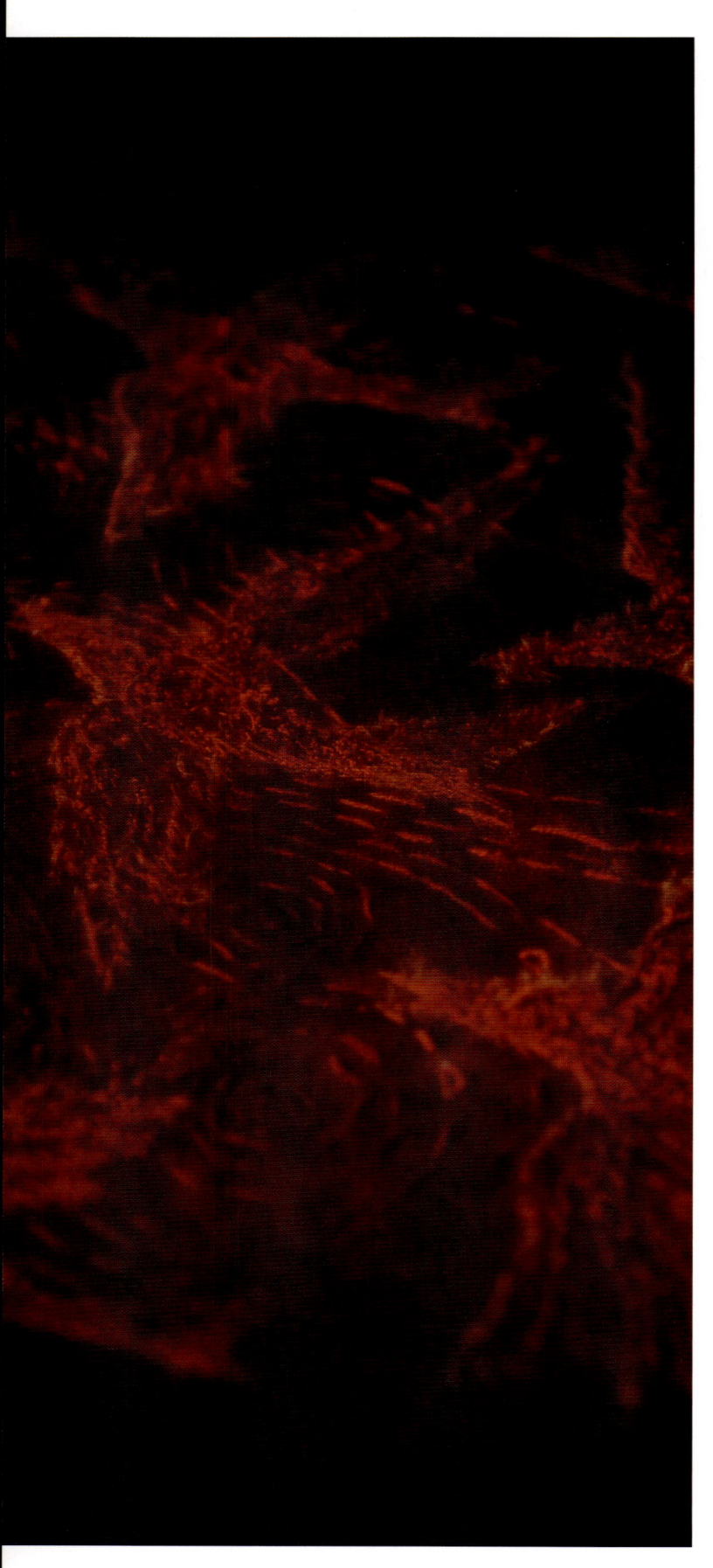

DARNING THE BLOODY CARPET

I began with the ground for the sparrows to lay on and for this I used a piece of leather that was a distressed oxblood colour as the base. I stitched several bird silhouettes with red machine thread on an invisible organza dyed a similar shade to the base leather. I cut the bird shapes out of the organza and arranged them randomly on the leather, further stitching into them with various red threads, creating a flow between them, with each shadow tracing their lives and connecting them.

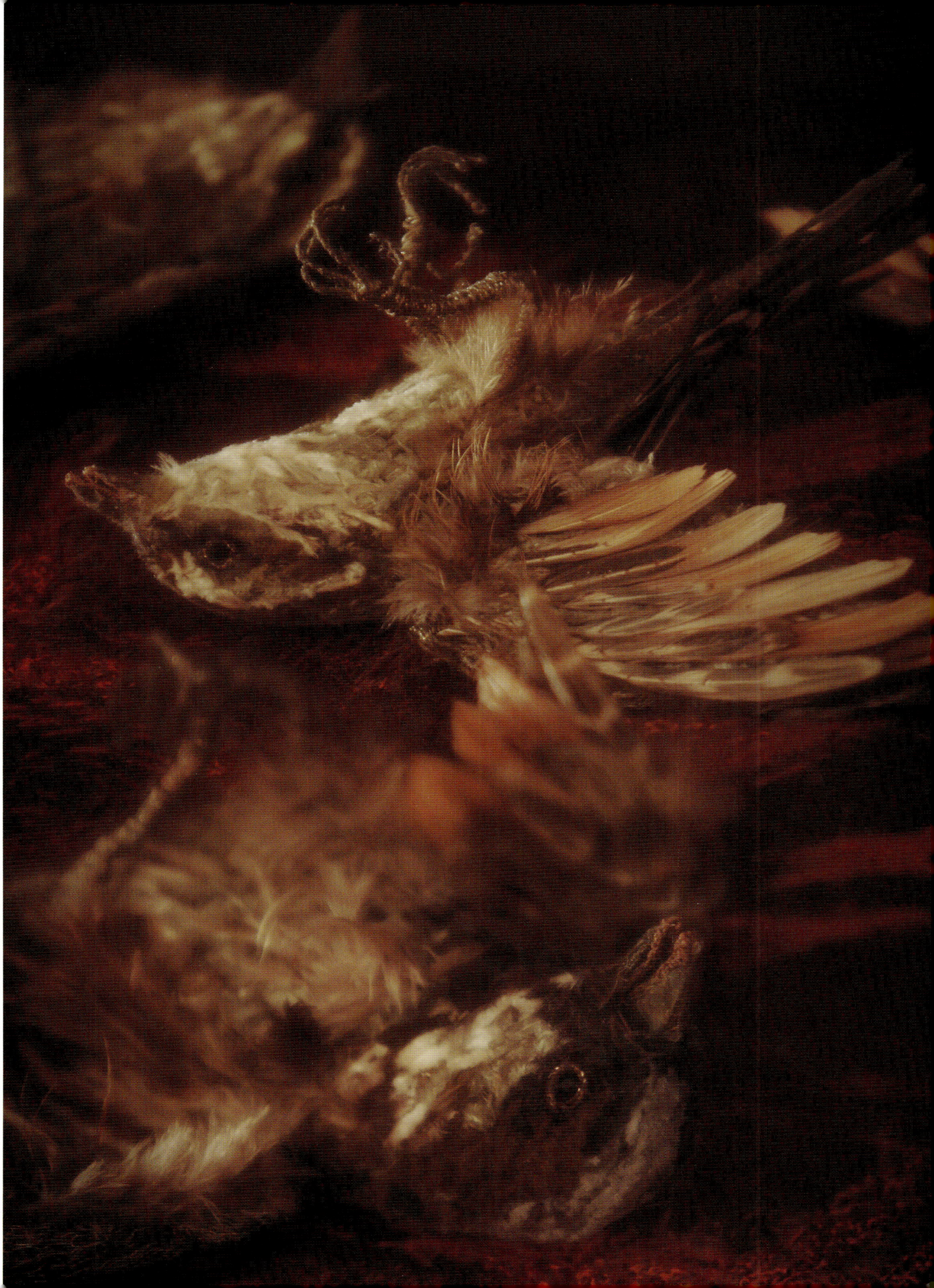

SCULPTING THE SPARROWS

Next I created the sparrows, for which I spent some time trying to photograph the sparrows in my garden (with limited success, of course!). When working on an embroidery, I do have an initial idea in my mind, but it will develop as I work on it. I use many different layers of materials and I start by gathering together all the threads, beads, wire and feathers etc. that I think may be useful to the piece, and then start to sketch my ideas out.

For these sparrows, I started by needle felting a basic shape. I don't work into it too much at this early stage, as I want to keep a softish shape that I can then sculpt as I stitch into it further when adding detail. Once I had the basic body shape and winglets formed, I encased the felt pieces in a tubular mesh wire – this neatens the shape and gives a base to stitch into.

For their beaks I backed a brown invisible organza with small shapes cut from a mother-of-pearl veneer with a 3M tape bonded to it, and then I used a fine wire on the edge, buttonholed around the shape with brown cotton machine embroidery thread. I wanted these little birds to be imperfect – slightly rough, tragic, sorrowful and forlorn-looking, so I used a variety of threads to create shape and stitch a suggestion of the patterning and feathers for each one. I found the cotton chenille threads to be particularly good for these sparrows and I also used some feathers threaded into the wings and tails to give them an echo of reality.

For the eyes I used a small faceted bead outlined with a dull grey metallic overdyed Kreinik braid. I created the claws and legs by twisting fine wire together for the shape and then wrapping these firstly with a fine silk Mori thread and then with a dull metallic overdyed Kreinik braid. I didn't fully stitch the wings on as I wanted the freedom to play around with the birds when positioning them on the red shadow carpet, so they are just pinned on ready to play their part in the tableau.

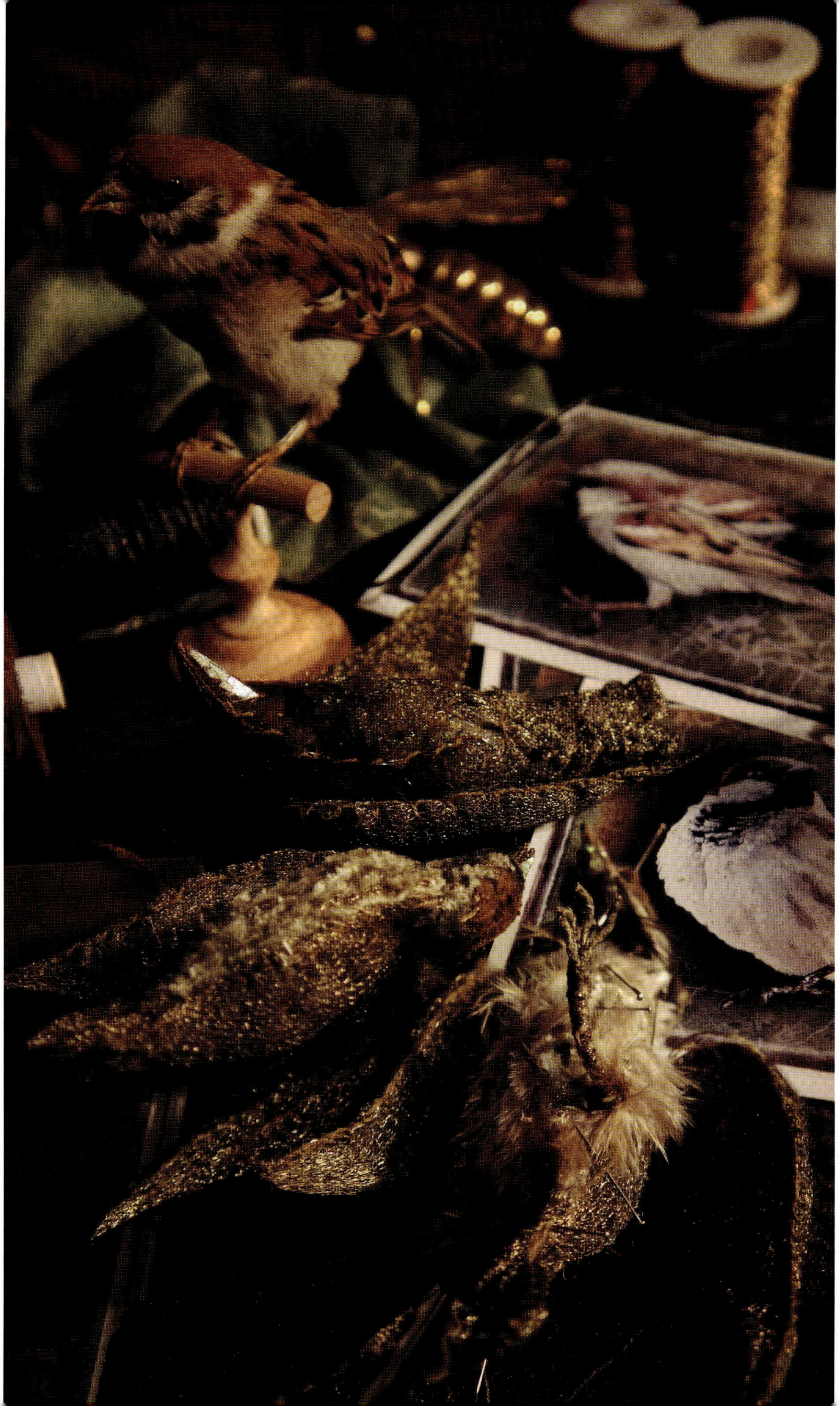

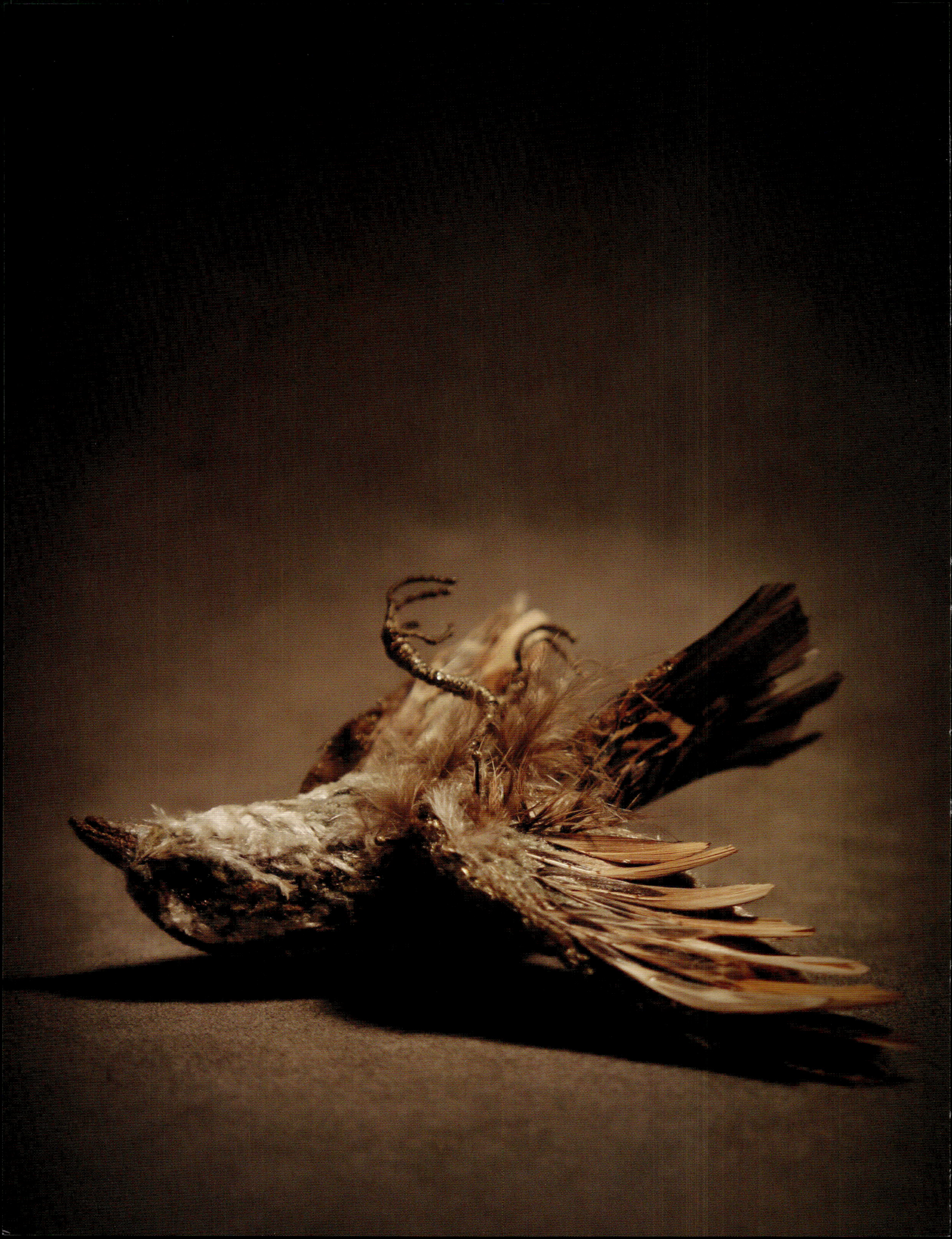

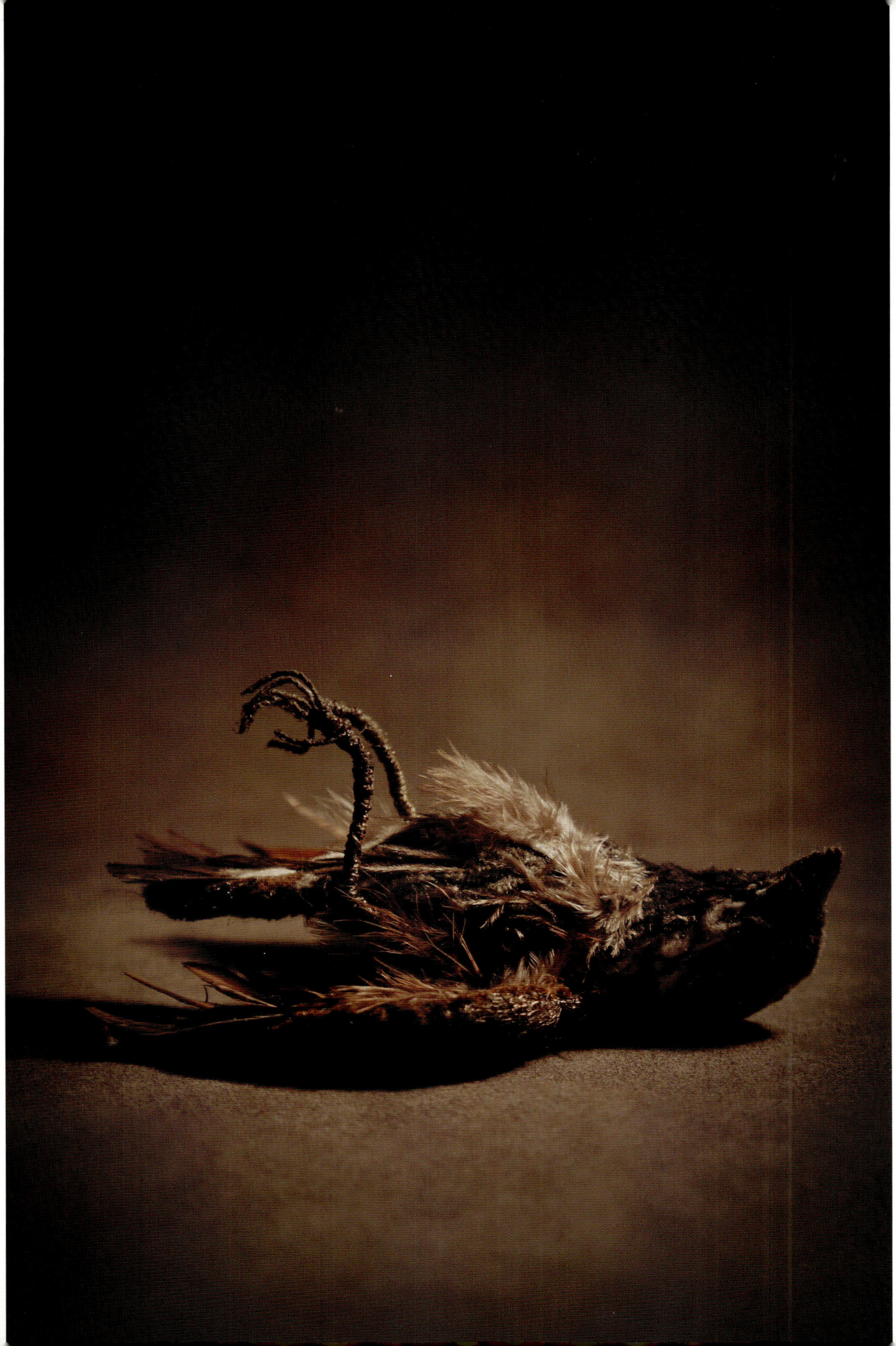

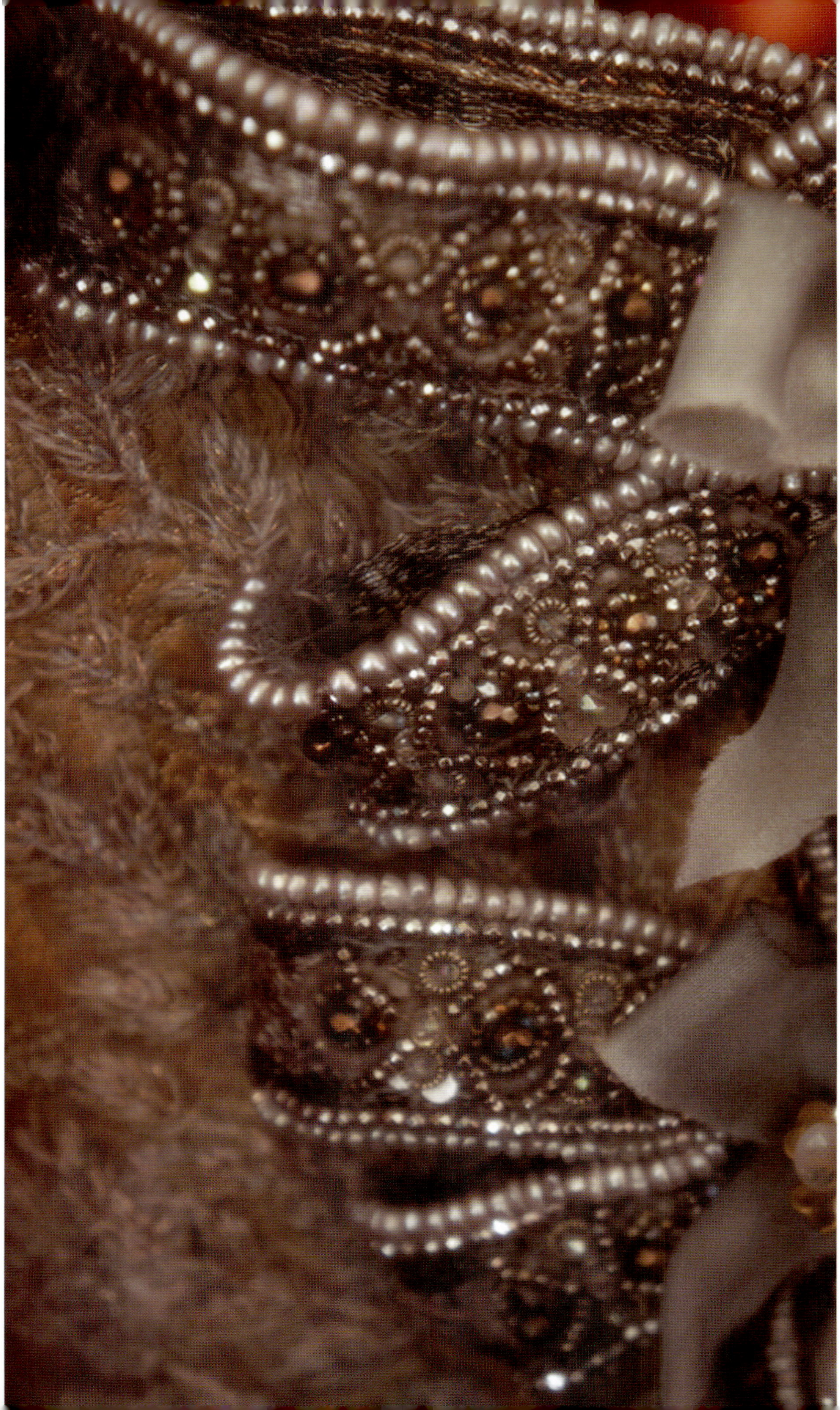

THE STOMACHER

I wanted the stomacher to be richly decorated, more like a jewellery piece, so I took inspiration from some design drawings that belong to The Cooper Hewitt Museum collections and also looked at various images of 18th-century jewellery pieces.

To realize this embroidery design I needed to make a base, then separately create the jewelled bows, before finally piecing it all together. I made the stomacher base shape from some blue linen backed onto a Jacobean linen twill, which is produced for The Crewel Work Company using flax grown in Scotland and has a wonderful honey colour. I had a length of vintage ribbon, which, because of the weave, had long floats on the back – this was the perfect colour for the base, over which I laid a filigree leaf embroidered section stitched onto silk crepeline. To either side I used a contemporary embroidered ribbon, which, again, I preferred the reverse of for my purpose. So this was the background onto which I attached the jewelled bows.

For the bows I stitched a silver mesh wire onto silk crepeline in my desired shape and outlined the edges with faceted hematite beads and small grey freshwater pearls. I then jewelled and beaded the bows using vintage sequins, Swarovski beads and flat backs. For the centres of the bows I used an Indian brass flower, some faceted moonstone drops wired together and a central faceted blue Czech glass bead to create a jewelled flower, with a grey drop pearl hanging from it, and set it on a small silk ribbon bow. Once I had created the 'flat' bows I then attached them to a central spine, jewelling and beading the top edge. I then laid this on top of the base and raised each bow element, attaching them in position on the base so that the bows sat away and were more three-dimensional.

As I wanted this stomacher to be decadent, ostentatious and dominant, I imagined the corset to be made from something almost invisible, and toyed with the idea of using acrylic rods instead of boning. Whilst looking for something suitable, as invisible boning doesn't yet exist, I came across a thermoplastic material that cosplayers use. This is a sort of plastic you can heat and mould into a variety of shapes, and it comes in a transparent form, which I thought would be useful for me to create an invisible bodice shape to photograph the corset and stomacher on. I watched many online tutorials and then had a go at shaping the Worbla TranspArt® around a mannequin shape I had... I take my hat off to those cosplayers who transform this into intricate shapes, as it turns out it isn't my forte! But I was able to create a rough shape that worked for my purpose, and the TranspArt® was also cut into strips to use as boning alongside the acrylic rods.

THE CORSET

For the corset itself I chose to contact a costume cutter/maker friend of mine, Margaret Pescott, who I met when working on *Game of Thrones* and with whom I collaborated on various costumes for the character Daenerys. Luckily for me she had a wee bit of spare time in between jobs and was up for the challenge. I probably could have attempted this myself but knew she would do a far better job than I could, particularly given the delicate fabrics being used, which most definitely required her highly skilled couture hands. The corset was made with a pale blue silk crepeline, lined in a soft grey silk crepeline. The edges were bound with Hanah silk ribbon, which is a bias habotai that has a random print and comes in many lovely shades. The boning was a combination of the strips of Worbla TranspArt® and pale blue, light-reflecting acrylic rods. I was so delighted when I opened up the parcel she sent – it is such a beautiful, delicate thing of loveliness, and absolutely perfect.

I now had all the elements to create my setting for the jewelled stomacher. I stitched the wonderful silk crepeline corset onto the TranspArt® shape and lined it with red acetate. I stitched the stomacher onto the front of the corset and added two red bows hanging down from the straps, with slightly tattered ends. The corset was then suspended over the bloody carpet of dead sparrows. The background was simply a dark brown dupion silk on a stretcher frame, which suited the style of the photography for this piece. I experimented with different stocking filters over the camera lens, which gave a more painterly feel, evoking something of the work of 18th-century still life artist Jean-Baptiste-Siméon Chardin.

The heart can be loving and caring, or cold and lacking empathy. For the subsequent artwork, *Entropy*, which was developed from *The Heart*, I wanted to weave in the themes of greed and overconsumption – of us bleeding the planet dry. Again, I would use colour palette and symbolism as well as the construction/display to portray this.

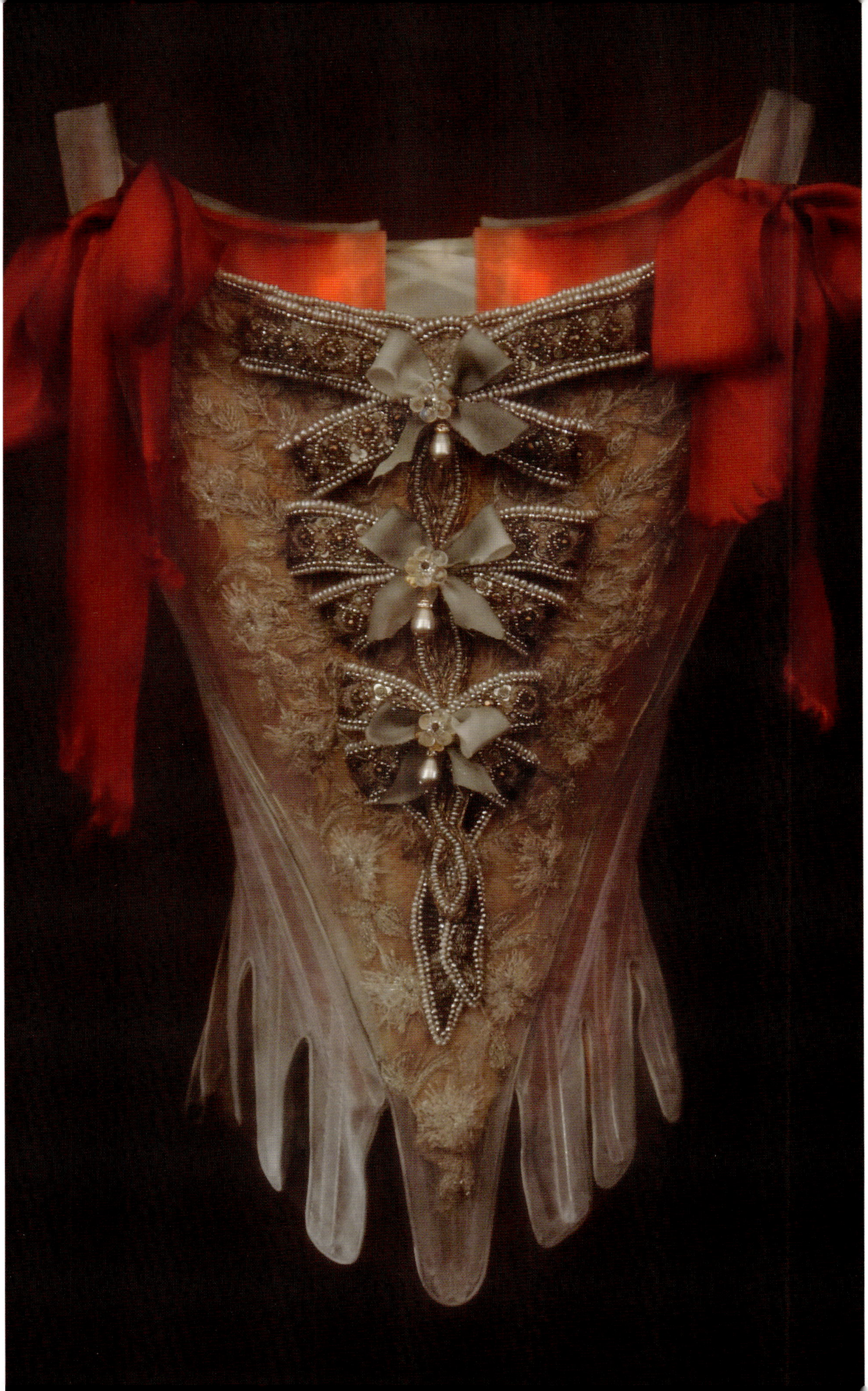

artwork insight
entropy

From the artefact *The Heart*, I developed and conceived the collection of works for *Entropy*. Again the colour palette would be key, but also the construction would be important in how it would be displayed. Red would be predominant as it is the colour of desire, the colour of blood that flows through us all, and an arresting colour that is a warning sign. Because of the Baroque designs of the 18th century, with their asymmetry, I wanted this piece to be different when viewed from either side. In my initial sketched ideas, one side shows decadent, beautiful, jewel-like birds with honeysuckle flowers between them, representing us sucking the life out of the planet, but later this developed and I set a stone heart between them, which is being struck by lightning that is streaking across a thunderous sky backdrop. When seen from the other side, we discover that these exotic birds have inner jewelled skeletons, representing how wealth stays with those who have it: despite uprisings and revolutions brought about by inequality and desperation, ultimately nothing much really changes. The background has a blue-grey sky with a bit of thunder creeping in, and a blood-butterfly cloud, jewelled with fireworks polluting the air. This relates to greed, inequality and how we are all complicit in overconsumption and the effect it is having on the world around us. The structure of this artwork is also reminiscent of the guillotine, as the piece is sliced in two.

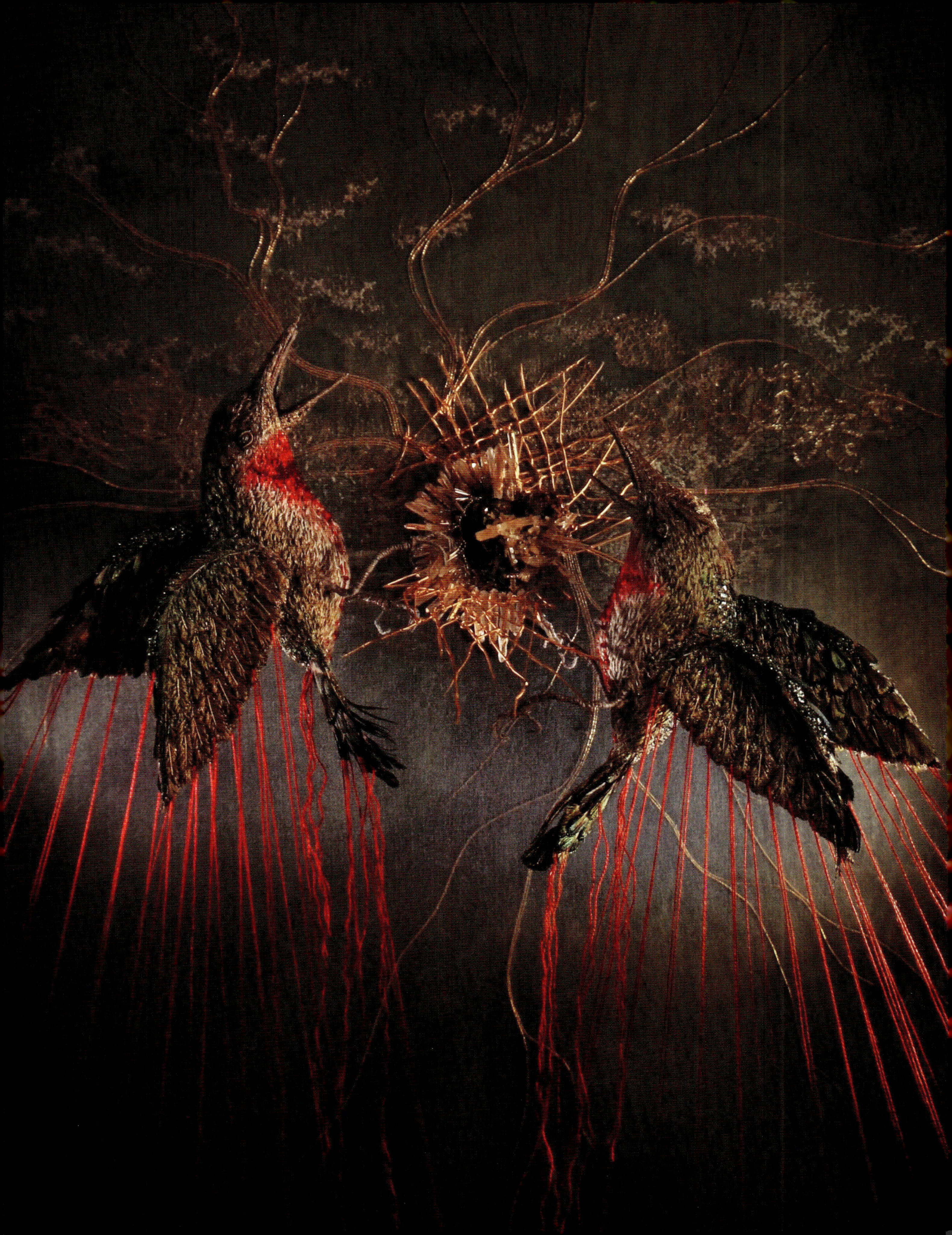

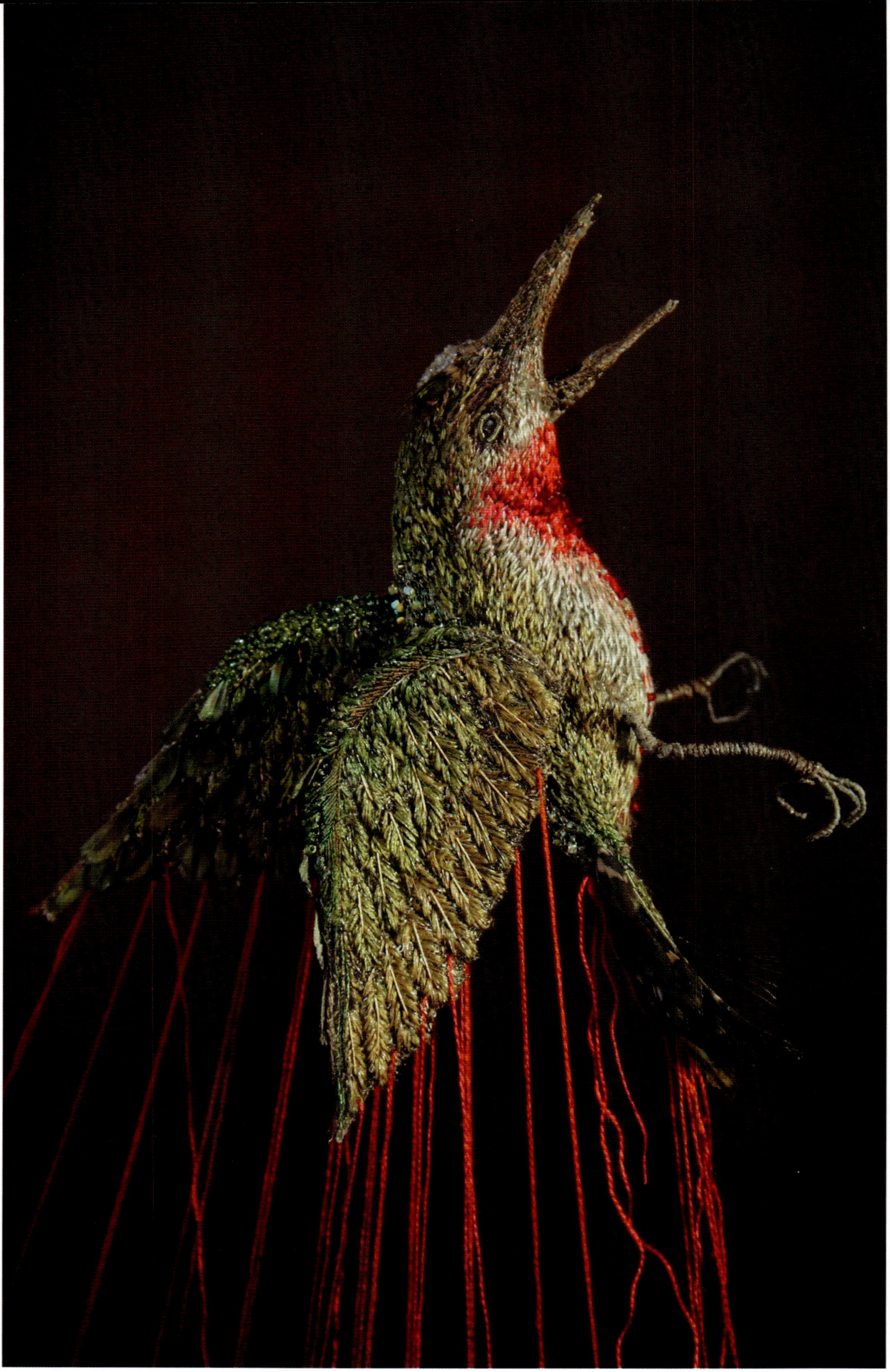

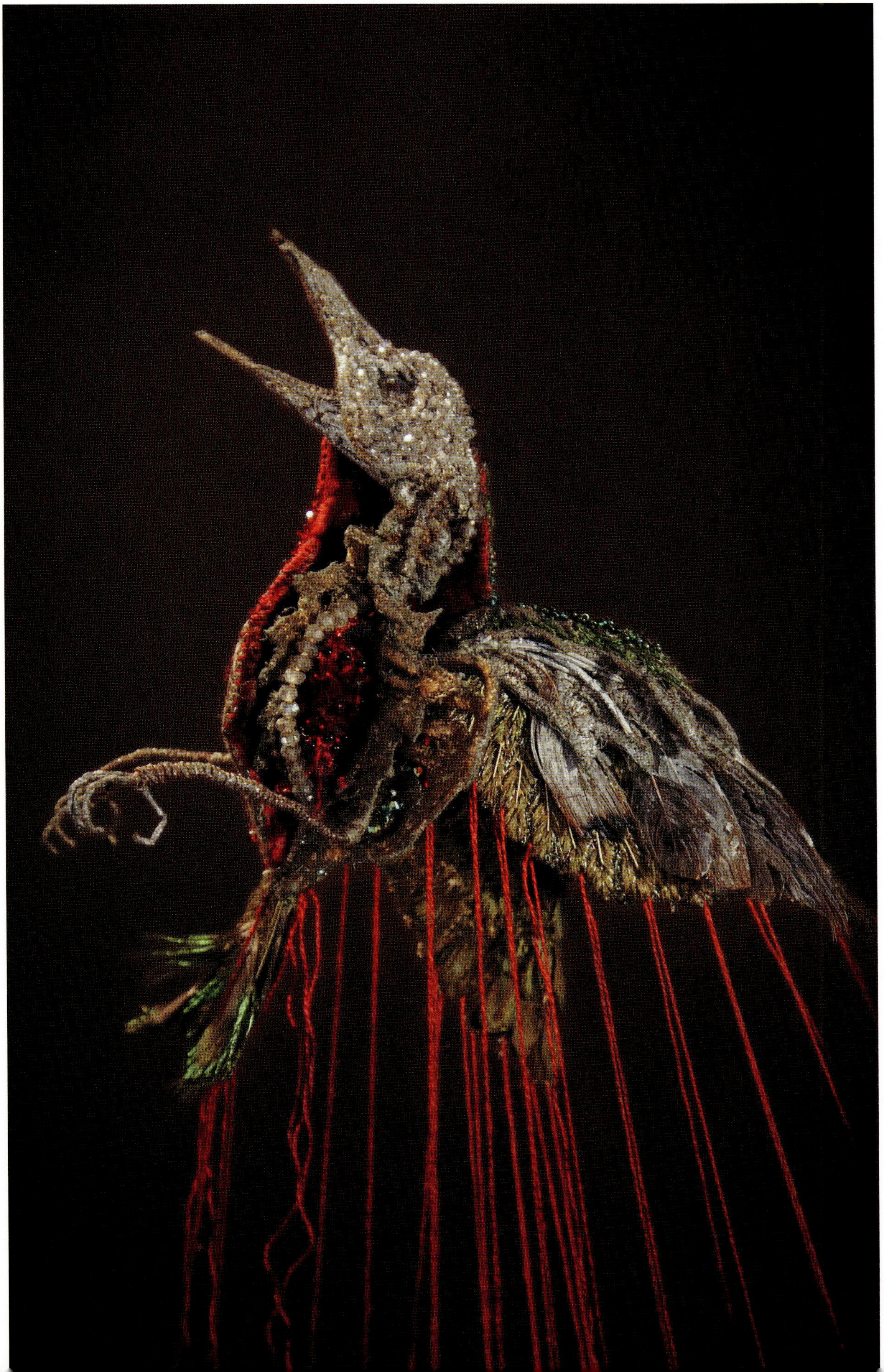

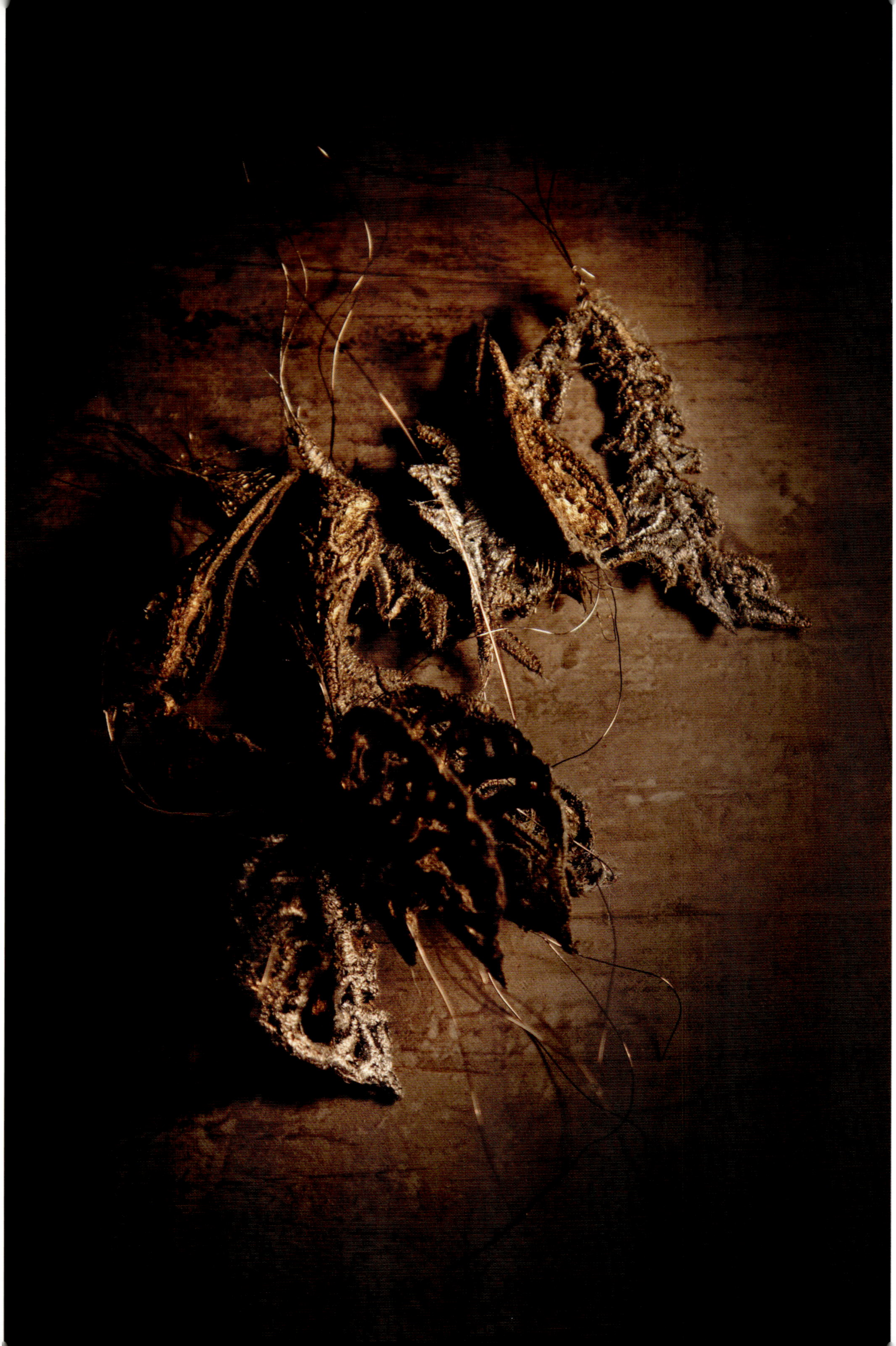

CREATING THE JEWELLED SKELETONS

I decided to start with the skeletons of the birds, and I wanted them to look as if they were gilded and jewelled as befitting these decadent specimens. I wasn't setting out to create an anatomically correct skeleton, merely something that reads to the eye as a suggestion of one. First, I had to think of the structure and sketch out my pattern pieces required to construct each element. I made separate shapes for the skull, spine and ribcage with dense embroidery and wired the edges of all of them. I rubbed silver-coloured Goldfinger into the stitching and used some stamping ink, embossing powder and a heat gun to create a gilded feel (see right). I beaded the skull with some small Swarovski crystals, used a faceted labradorite gemstone behind the eye and small labradorite beads for the spine. I then assembled the pieces to create my bird skeleton.

For the wing I again used wired embroidered shapes, with feathers coated with stamping ink and embossing powder, melted with a heat gun to give a silvered effect. Once the skeletons were taking shape I moved on to the half bird carcasses.

SCULPTING THE HALF BIRDS

To create the initial shape I used needle felting, making a basic hollowed shape, which I covered with mesh wire and then used jet AB2X Swarovski beads along the back to give some iridescence. I laid more wire over the top to knock them back a touch and smooth the shape. I then stitched into the head and body with various threads to sketch in some detail and shape the birds, adding some tiny red jewelled Swarovski beads, dripping down from the colour at the neck, to echo the executions of the French revolution.

I threaded some small peacock feathers into the tail and wings. The carcass was lined with red velvet and I made a small red jewelled piece on illusion tulle to insert as the heart. Whilst making the carcass, I had to keep checking that the skeleton would fit inside it snugly, so that it would fill the shape and help the bird take form. I attached the wings and one leg to the carcass, blending over the joins with more stitching, shading into the bird. I then fixed the skeleton into the shape, attaching the second leg to this and inserted the jewelled red heart.

113

BLOOD-BUTTERFLY PRINT BACKGROUND

As a backdrop for the jewelled skeletal birds I wanted a blue-grey sky colour with a band of red streaking across it. I started by creating a blood splatter pattern on mounting board with red Indian ink. I tried to do the same on fabric but the bleed was too soft, so I decided my best route would be to be to work from the Indian ink on board and do some Photoshop® manipulation which could then be digitally printed on fabric.

I also experimented with the print on acetate. I thought I could print onto acrylic, laser-cut the bird silhouettes and attach my jewelled birds to them to give the effect of the birds in mid-air rather than using strings (this is something for further down the line, as initially I will be using the birds as props and create different settings to photograph them in from either side). Whilst playing with the acetate print, I laid it over a butterfly print and that sparked the idea for the blood-butterfly print. This still had the feel of a blood-stained sky as a backdrop to the jewelled fireworks that would sit behind the skeleton birds.

Once I had finalized my print, I sent it off to the lovely team at CAT Digital. I have limited experience with digital fabric printing, but have already found that it can be tricky to get the exact colour you want. As different fabrics react very differently with the same print, it is best to do a test first and try out different fabrics to get close to what you want. I had this print made on cotton satin as well as on silk organza, as I thought I might want to layer the design. When they arrived back I was pleased with the result as sometimes reds can come out a bit too punchy for me on silk, but these looked great. My only issue was that the blue background was too pale and not as gloomy as I wanted, so I tried using some Dye-Na-Flow ink, wetting the prints then brushing and water spraying into it, which kind of worked but wasn't perfect. As I had repeats of the design I thought I would try dyeing it in a pot on the stove. I wasn't sure how it would affect the red, but thought it was worth a shot, and luckily for me it worked really well and gave me that slightly moody sky I was after.

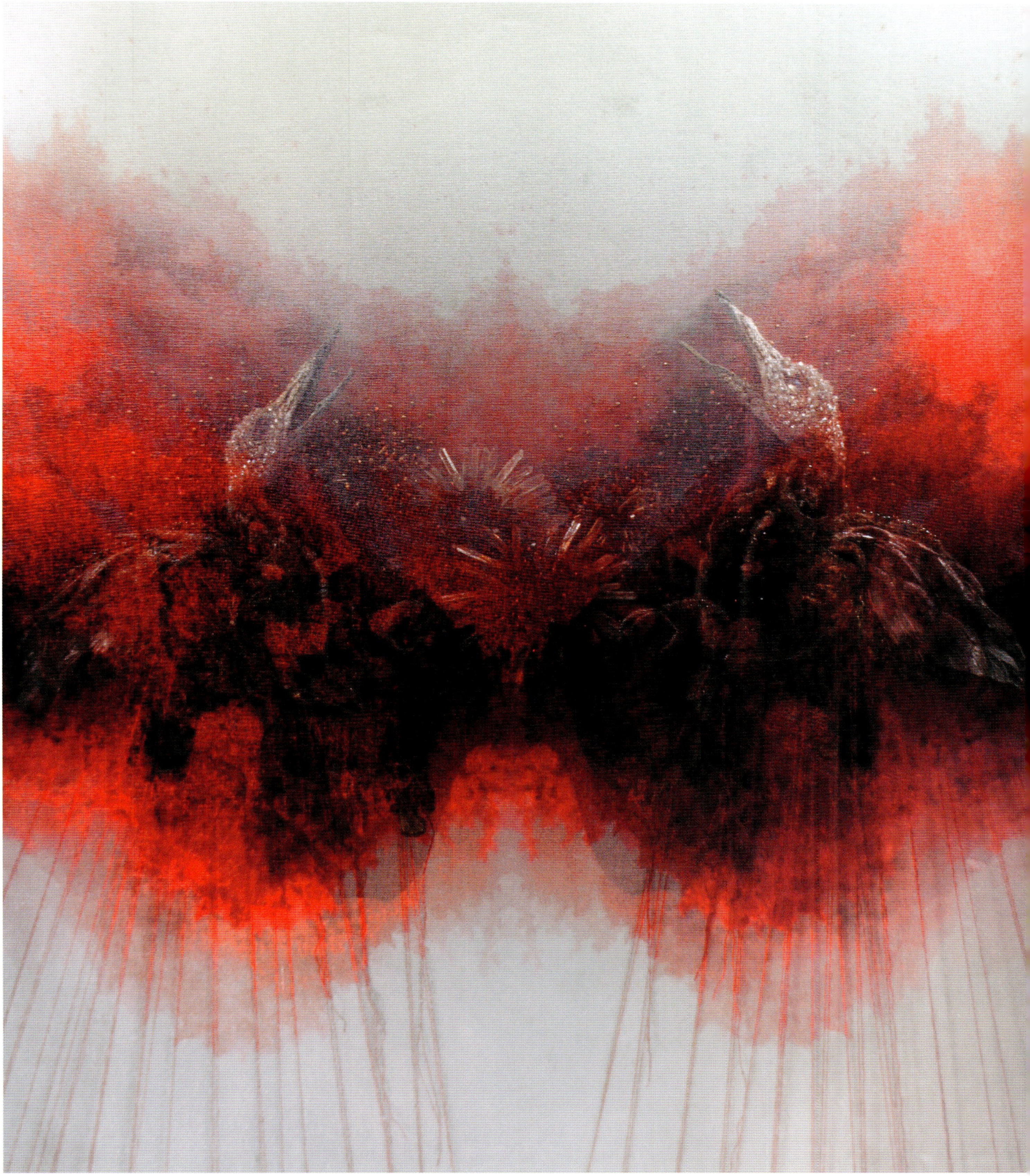

JEWELLING THE FIREWORKS

For the skeletal side of this artwork I imagined the blood-butterfly background as a warning sign, with jewelled fireworks bursting across this bloody, polluted sky. For the larger bursts I used some fine crystal quartz needle points, which I couched down on grey illusion tulle in a circular form and then I glued over the stitching on both sides to hold it firm. I created many smaller jewelled firework bursts, by embroidering the shapes onto red tulle, using a red embroidery thread and adding small Miyuki seed beads along the fine lines of the bursts. For the centres I used Swarovskis and some faceted garnet marquise beads – on some I also added tiny gold faceted French steel cut beads and fine gold bugles. Once beaded, I cut these pieces out from the tulle, adding them to the centre of the quartz circles and arranging others around them. I stitched them to the background, adding more of the fine French steel cut beads to blend the tulle cut-outs onto it, creating my firework backdrop.

The blood-butterfly sky bejewelled with fireworks was set as the backdrop and I then strung the skeletal side of the birds in front of this using a Perspex frame with holes drilled around the edge. I used a fine bead thread to secure them from their heads to the top of the frame (these would be digitally edited out later). Using a red embroidery thread, I secured the birds in position, painting lines flowing from their wings attaching to the acrylic frame below – these would give the effect of the sky raining blood. I did many test shots and really liked the effect when I added another layer of the blood-butterfly print on organza fabric in front of the embroidered birds. This diffused the image and gave a more painterly feel, which looked as if the sky was on fire with plumes of red, leaving the skeletal birds gasping for air.

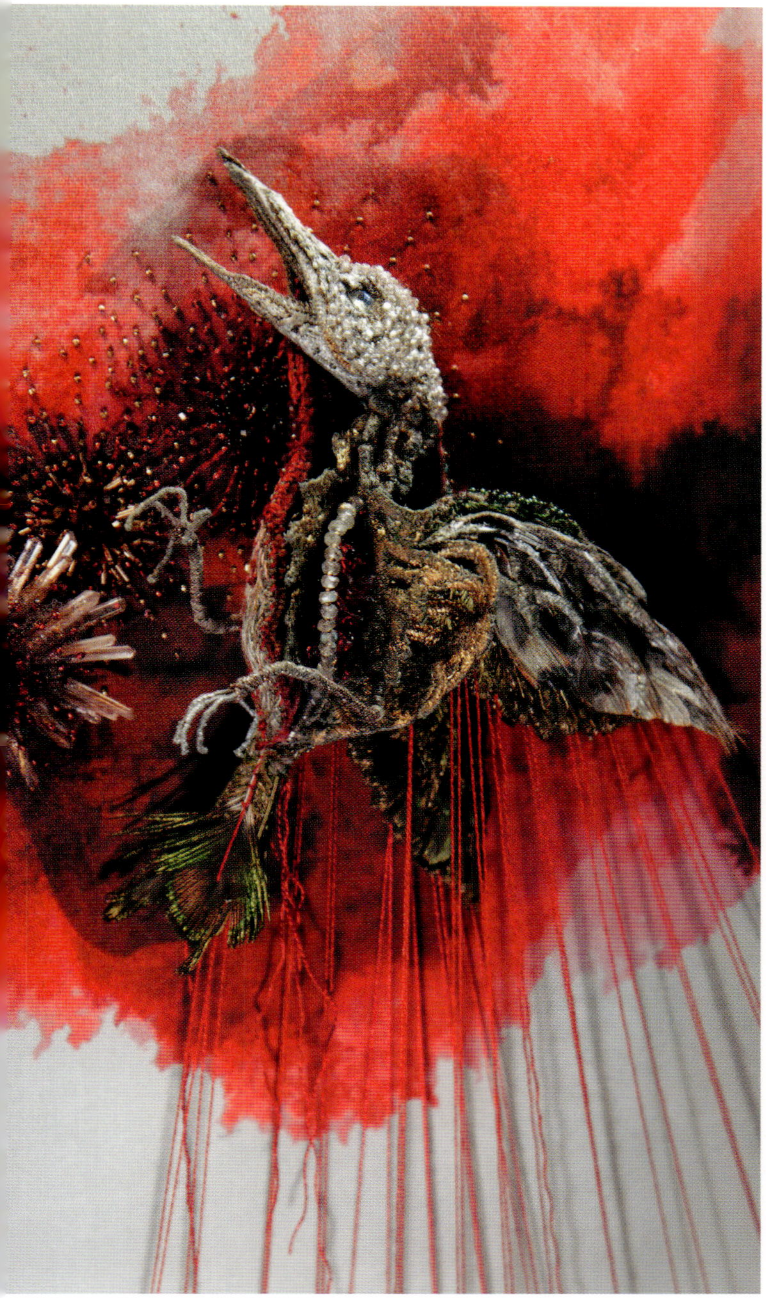

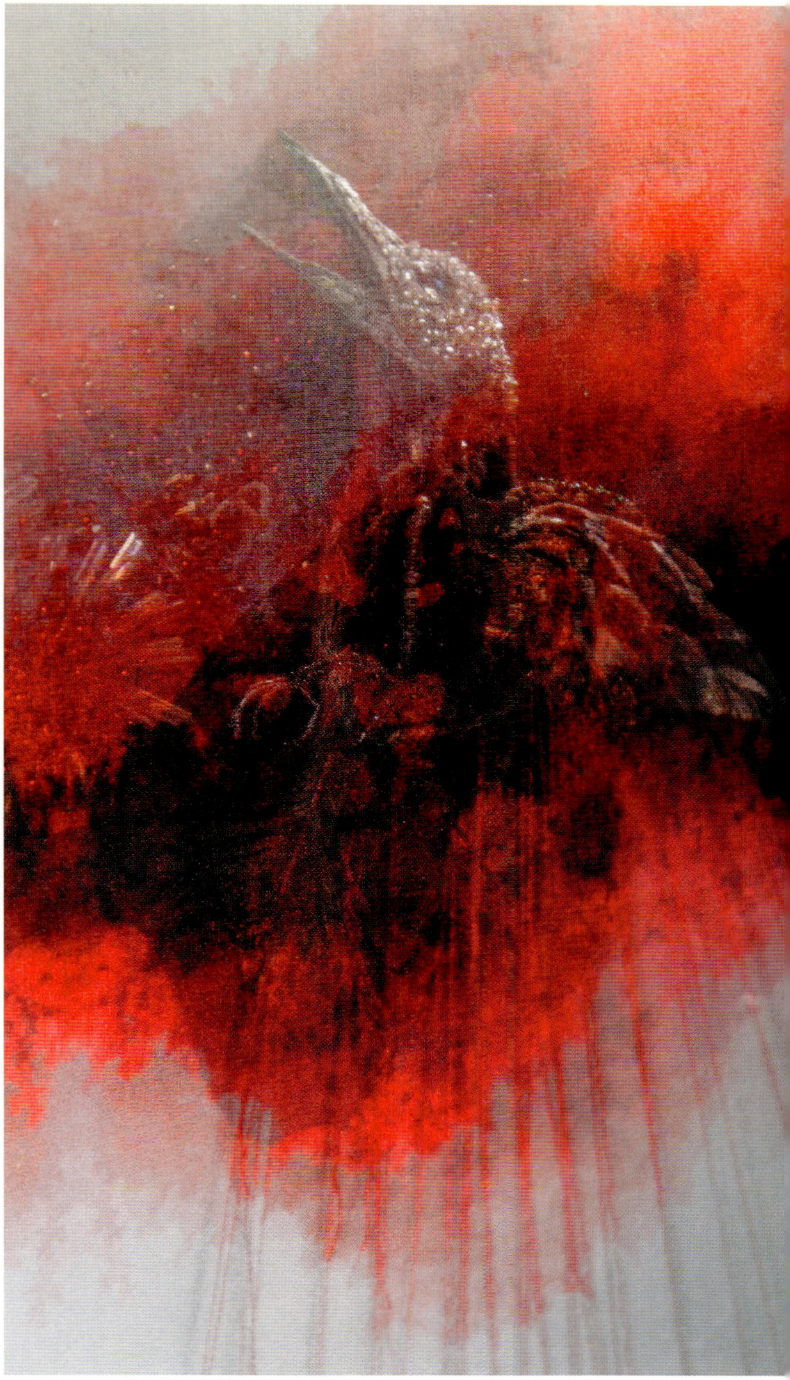

CREATING THE HONEYSUCKLE

Although ultimately this piece never appeared as part of the final compositions for *Entropy*, I thought I would still show you the branch of honeysuckle that I created and an insight into how I made it. For the honeysuckle, I needed to make each trumpet in upper and lower sections, for which I embroidered the shapes on grey illusion tulle and wired the edges, before cutting them out and stitching together. These trumpets needed stamens, which I made using a thick buttonhole-type thread with a Miyuki delica glued at each end. This is a bit fiddly, but you just need to prepare your space and have a small washing line ready to hang the stamens over once the beads are glued to let them dry; once dry, you can snip off any excess glue. If you want finer stamens, use a finer thread, but bear in mind that this may then need stiffening. You could dip the ends in an acrylic paint rather than using beads, try using wax or source something pre-made. I tend to look for vintage versions of stamens, as they are a bit more subtle and refined, but it depends on how you want the finished look to be – bold or fine, there is always a solution.

Along with the main open trumpets I also made some of the inner 'starburst' petals, again by embroidering on the illusion tulle and wiring the edges before cutting them out. For the centre base of each bloom I knot stitched with mesh wire on some illusion tulle and created a little dome for the petals to nestle in. I couched a ring of opal beads on the mesh wire dome and dotted more of the opals in the centre. I am often drawn to opals in their many forms – these are quite a dark, muddy yellow but the iridescence shines subtly in the light.

I inserted the central starburst petals, and in between created some bead petals with Swarovski golden-shadow faceted round beads attached with a red beading thread to add subtle colour. I cut this central piece out of the tulle and then attached the trumpets around the outside. I twisted all of the wire ends from the petals together to create the stem, added some sprigs of yellow beads on gold wire that I thought helped to age it, and then wrapped green thread around the wires to finish the stems. I made one open main flower, some semi-open buds and some leaves in the same way as before. Once you have all the pieces, it is a matter of arranging these elements to suit and tidying the joins by wrapping threads around them. Although I often embroider onto silk crepeline dyed to match what the piece will be applied to, for this I found the illusion tulle was better as the back and front look fairly similar, even if you haven't done your neatest stitching. After reviewing the photographs of the jewelled birds with honeysuckle, I decided the colour palette wasn't quite right and didn't fit with its opposing image. So I decided to create a new backdrop to photograph them in front of and chose to eliminate the honeysuckle centre.

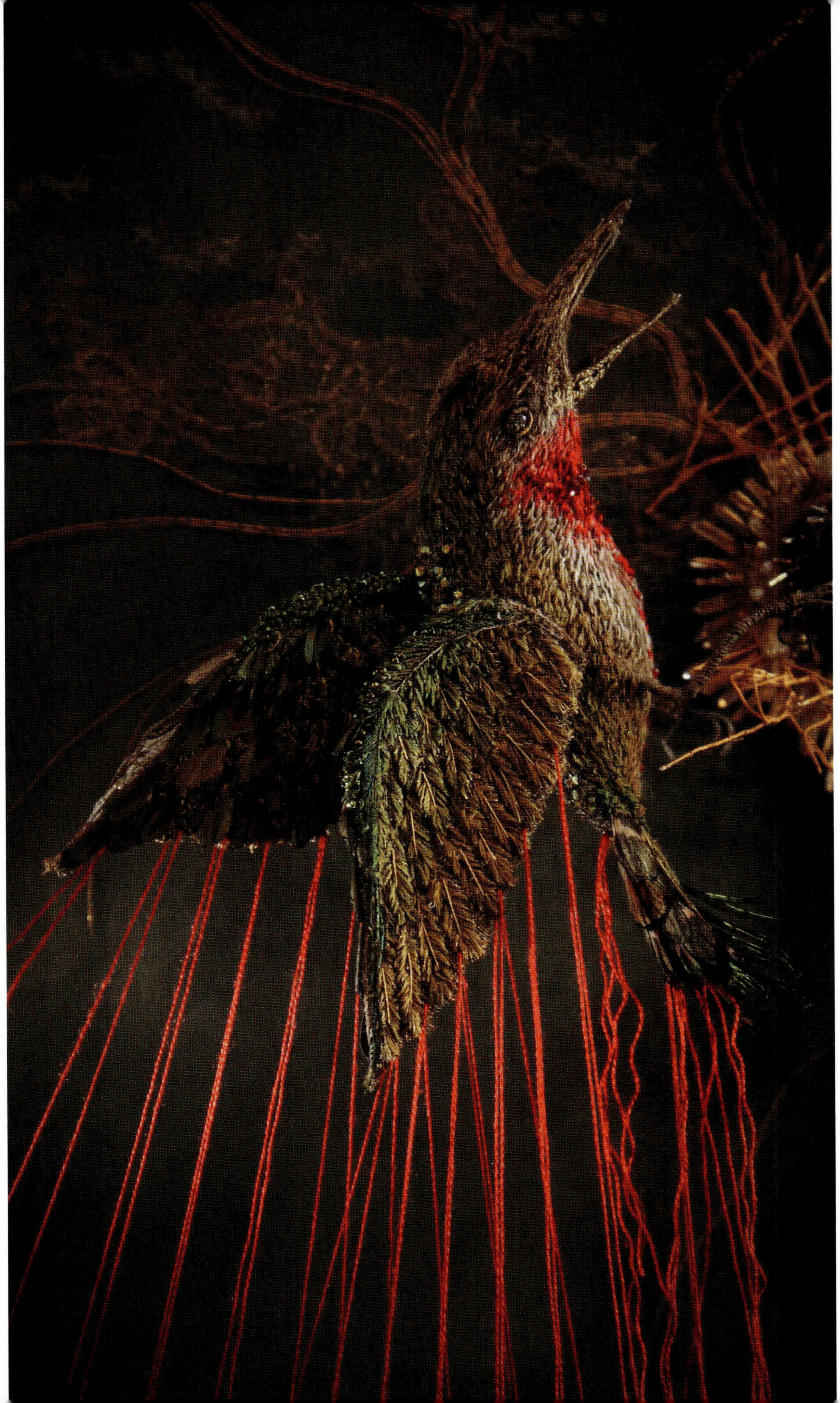

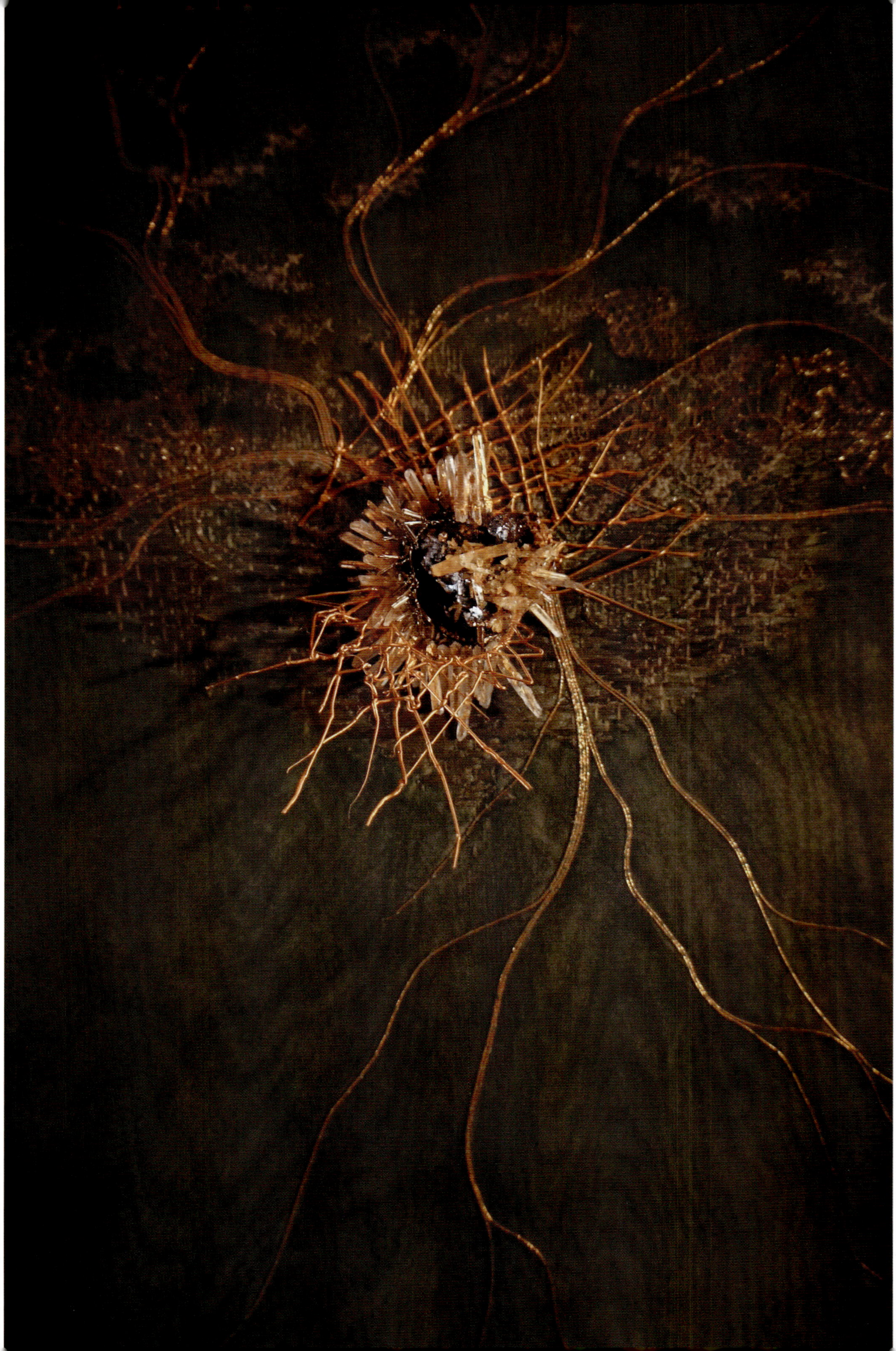

THE STONE HEART

I had bought a heart-shaped mineral specimen I thought may suit this artwork, comprised of siderite, hematite and quartz. As it was too delicate to be drilled I needed to create a setting for it that would enable me to string it between the birds. To do this, I added some quartz matchstick points, creating more of a starburst to it. I didn't want the setting to be too pretty as I wanted to create a sense of foreboding in the background. I wanted it to look like a thunderous sky streaked with lightning.

I started with a blue taffeta layer, into which I darned and embedded organza to create a cloud-like pattern. I then couched down a gold Japan thread randomly to create the lightning streaks. I placed the birds in front of the backdrop and liked the lower red thread blood trails, so kept those and strung the stone heart in place. To get a bit more movement in the lightning, I created some fine filigree pieces with a three-dimensional printing pen in clear filament and sprayed them gold. I stitched some of these to the backdrop and fixed one to the front of the heart as if it was bursting from it. This now had much more of the mood and feel I was after for this side of the artwork.

I also created further explorations for this artwork using one of the sparrows in front of the blood-butterfly sky, with jewelled bloody roots trailing down underneath (see pages 41–43).

the head

"... you are free to choose, but not free from the consequences of your choice."
Anonymous

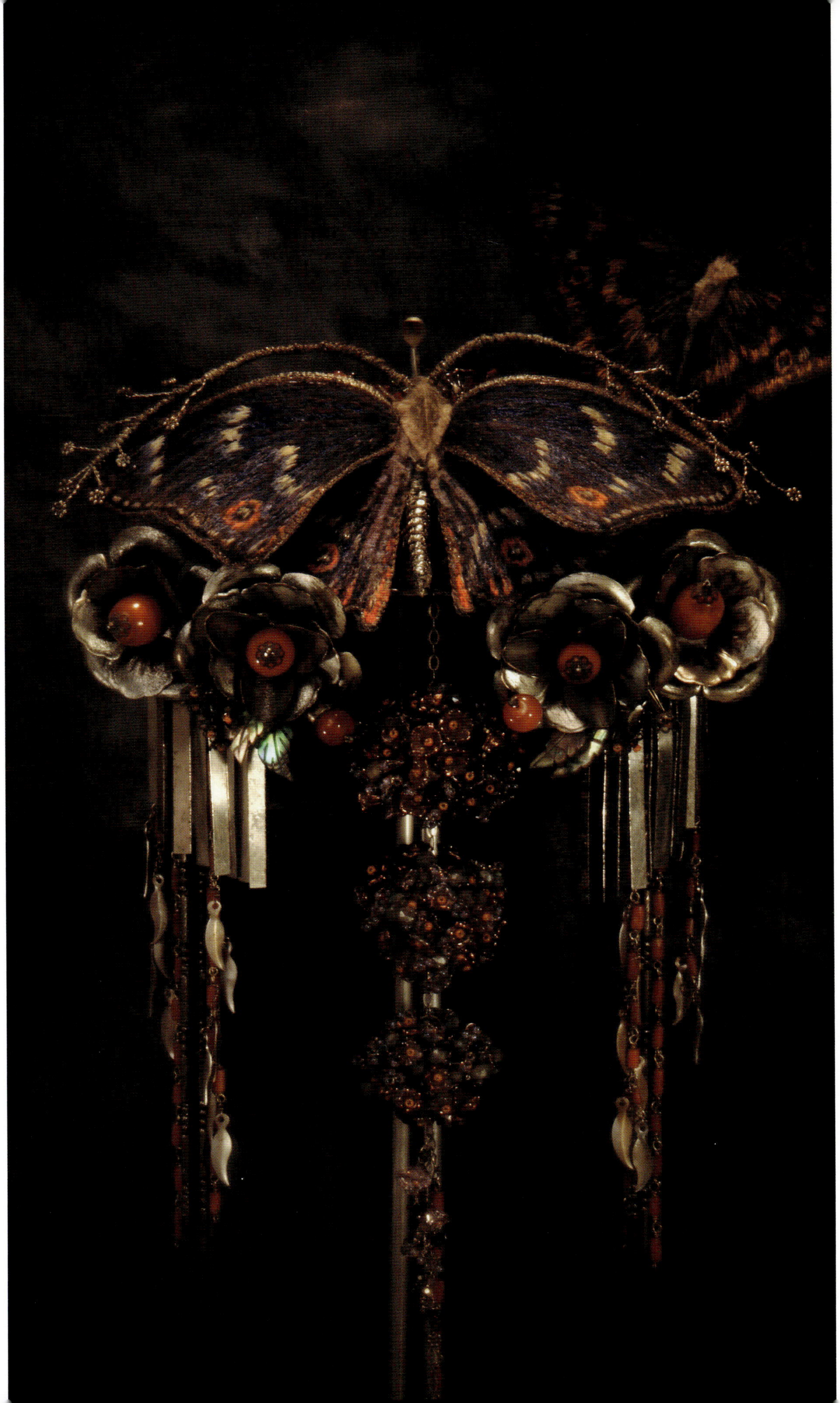

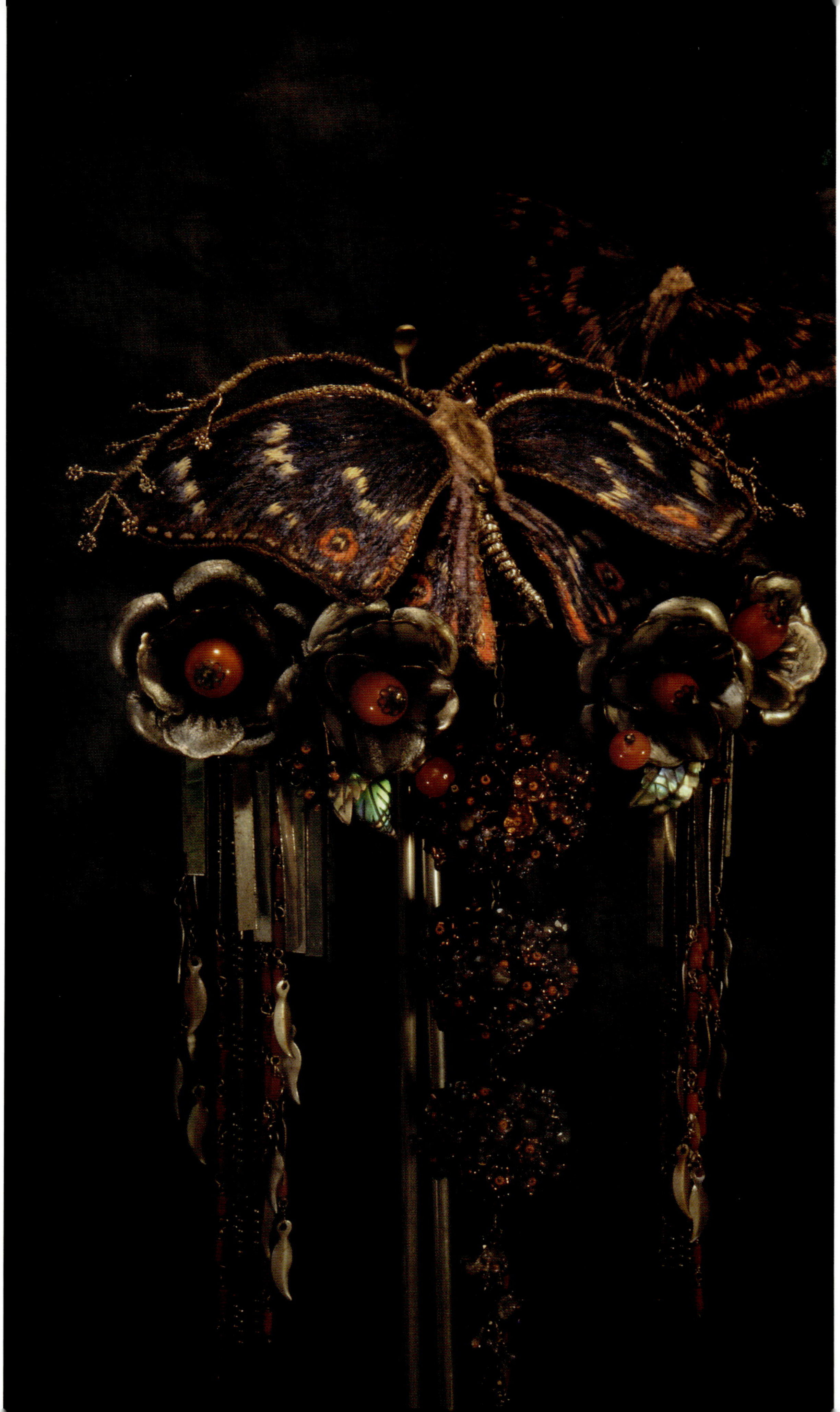

artefact insight
the head

The third artefact is a Japanese hairpin (*kanzashi*) from the late 19th century Meiji era. During this period the Japanese people became heavily influenced by the West, moving from being an isolated feudal society to an industrialized nation state. This saw them embrace a new revolution that was sweeping in from the West and continued at a pace around the world, creating wealth for many but social problems and poverty for others. The consequences for us and the environment from this global industrialization are clear to see, and the way forwards is ours to shape.

The *kanzashi* is a love token worn entangled in the hair, binding one to another; with the gift giver and recipient woven together. For the hairpin I wanted to use a butterfly motif and chose the purple emperor, as it is a rare sight these days. I do remember seeing them as a child near the copse at the back of the stables I spent most of my time at, but I haven't been lucky enough to catch sight of one more recently. A purple butterfly as an omen can represent being released from a burden, if you face a difficult or important issue, while the peonies surrounding the butterfly are symbols for living a peaceful and good life. The *kanzashi* has a background setting of a dark cloudy sky, denoting our lack of clarity, clouded vision, a masking of the truth and loss of moral conscience. The pin is skewered in a frozen lake that is starting to crack, showing our fragility and suggesting we should tread carefully to find the right path.

THE PEONIES AND BUDDLEJA

I used various beads, chains and metal flowers to create the decorative peony sprigs, with amber and carnelian beads for the flower centres. For the dangles I bought some ready-made *kanzashi* flutters that I dipped in antiquing fluid. I added to the flutters with some silver chain, a carnelian bead chain and some small brass Indian sequins.

I wanted to create a series of central dangling buddleja flowers that the butterfly is nestled on, which hangs down between the peony flutters. I made each flower ball of the buddleja by creating individual bead flowers with wire and twisted these together; I then linked each ball with fine silver chain.

BACKDROP

I used a dark blue fabric backdrop that has been dip-dyed, and as the fabric took the dye unevenly it has created a midnight sky with cloud drifts. This is one of those happy accidents when sometimes you haven't mixed the dye properly, or the fabric hasn't been fully rinsed before dropping it in the dye pot and the dye takes unevenly. I always keep these pieces as I know I will find a purpose for them.

CREATING THE BUTTERFLIES

For the main butterfly that is part of the hairpin, I painted a guide on some silk crepeline and then sketched and embroidered the detail with fine silk floss. I wired the edge of each wing to help hold the shape when attached to the body. As this is a jewellery-type piece, I wanted a tarnished metallic feel for the body and feelers. I kept the tail looking more metallic, but added some chenille thread and tiny feathers for the upper body section, with faceted crystals for eyes.

For the smaller butterflies, which I wanted to look as if they are taking flight from the hairpin, I used a similar technique to the blue butterflies on *The Hand* (see page 72). I printed a suitable butterfly image on a sheet of inkjet organza and embroidered over the printed image. The bodies were made from a fine lucet cord, with chenille thread nestled where the wings join the body. The eyes are 2mm Swarovski-faceted crystals and I used a fine, stiffened thread for the feelers.

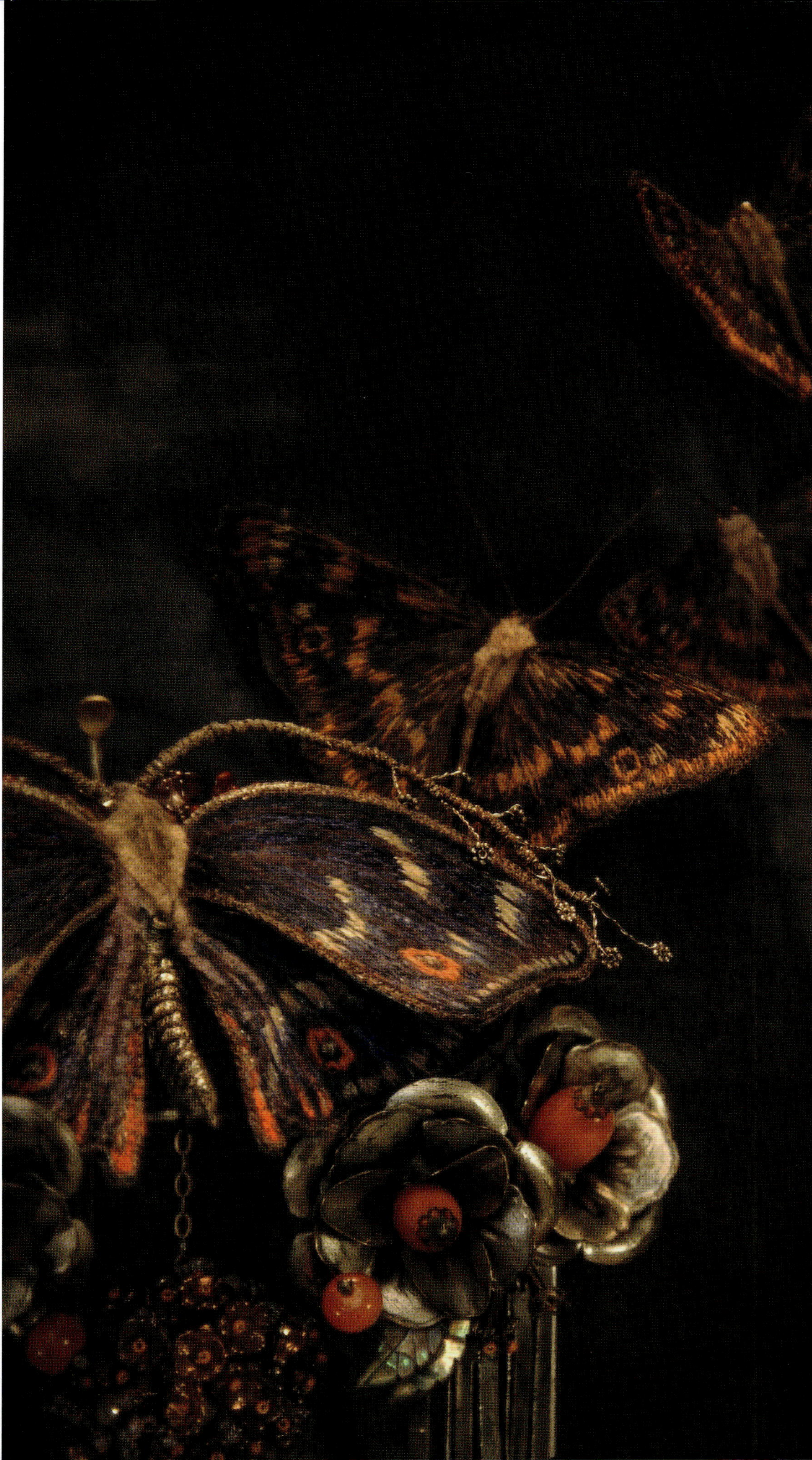

THE FROZEN LAKE FLOOR

I wanted the hairpin to be skewered into a frozen lake, with the ice cracking around it. The fragility of life and our ecosystem is plain to see but our vision is often clouded and it can be hard to decipher the truth: there are differing viewpoints on any one thing, depending on what best suits that individual. We have become less symbiotic and more parasitic as a species.

The base is a vinyl floor tile that has a silver copper patina effect. Over this I laid an invisible organza on which I embroidered the cracking of the ice and added some mother-of-pearl butterfly shapes integrated into the design of the frozen lake (see left).

I wanted to use the gloomy mood and dark colour palette I had been playing with from this artefact in the subsequent artwork *Conscience*, as well as using the layering and darning present in the Boro textiles of Japan as the underlying technique.

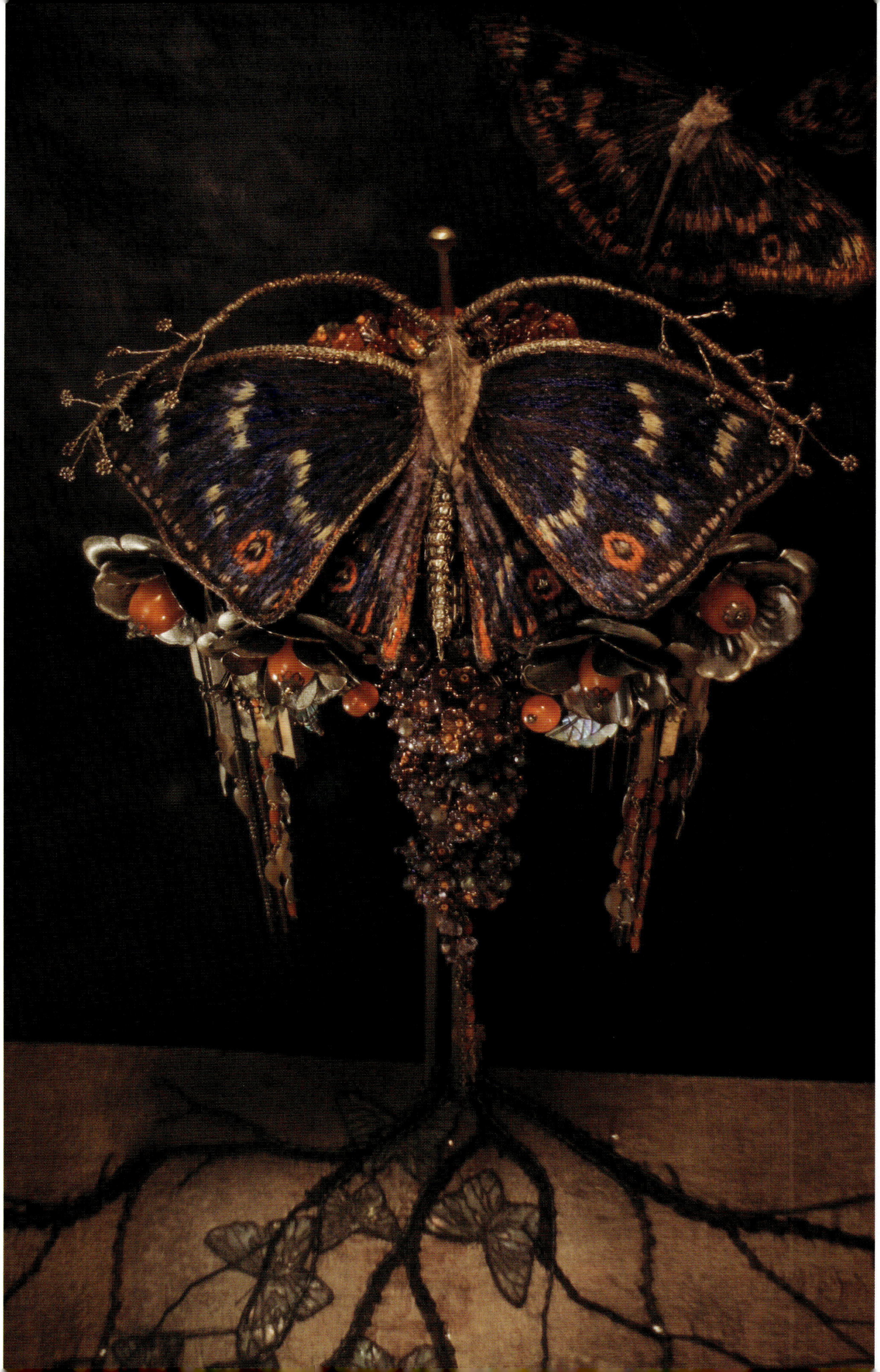

artwork insight
conscience

The Boro textiles of Japan were born out of poverty, stitched and layered together from generation to generation. They gave warmth and protection, preserving life and connecting those generations. These were my inspiration and I wanted to echo them in the layering and construction of this piece. I wanted to create a backdrop of a deep, dark lake, with reflections of shadow starlings in murmuration across the sky. Starlings can work together in harmony or be destructive and bullying. This dark watery chasm is interrupted by a blue streak – a kingfisher bursting from the lake.

The dark lake and background suggest our clouded vision, and losing touch with what is most important; but they also represent how we are still engulfed in an unpredictable future, facing the depths of despair. But out of that gloom the kingfisher is a glimmer of hope flashing by, leaving a trail to follow. The starlings flying in unison, working together as one unit.

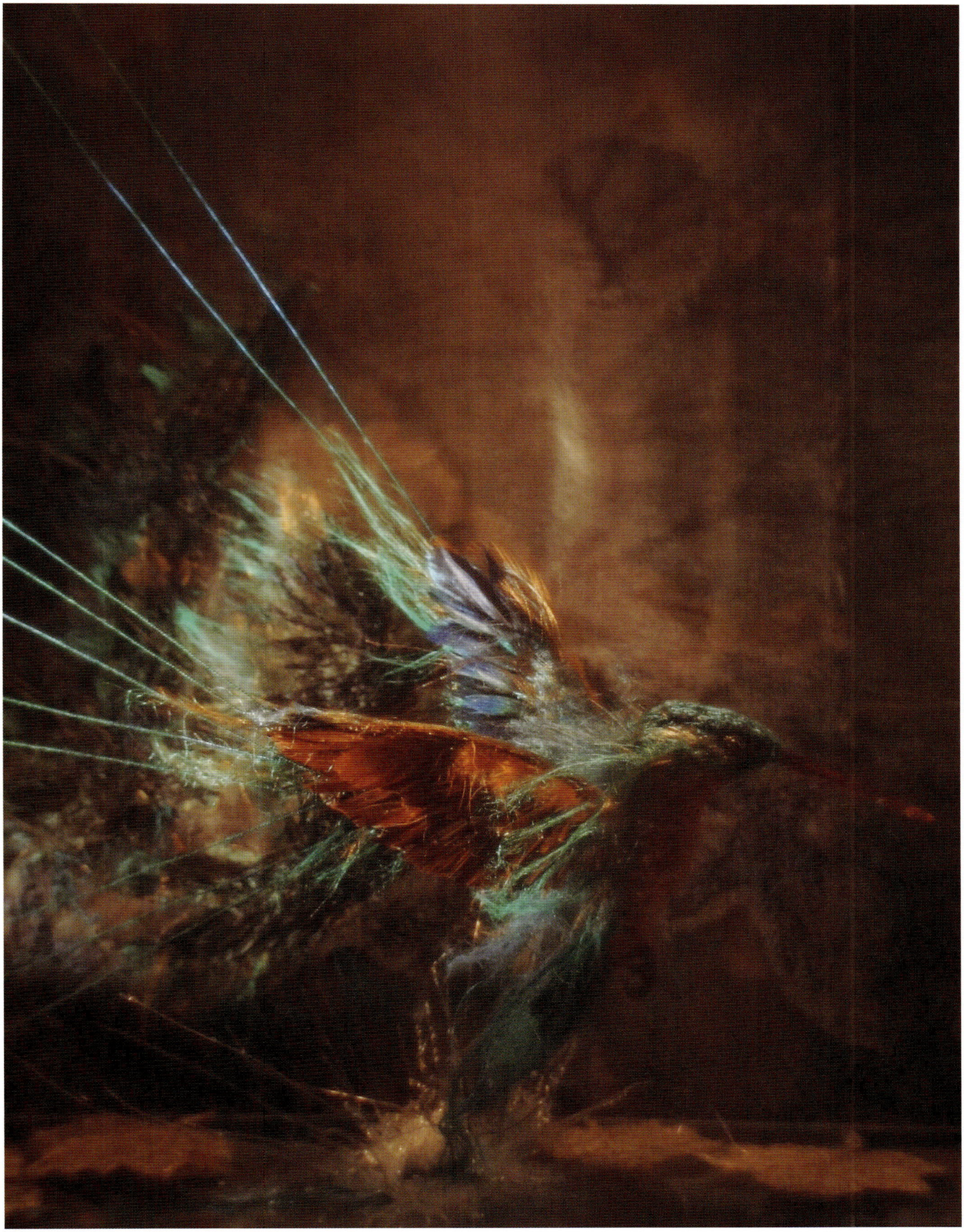

BACKGROUND

For the background board I started with a Perspex sheet that I covered with black oxidized metal leaf and patches of silver blush marbled leaf. For the background detail laid over the metal leaf, I created a trail of shadow birds, starlings in flight, a rough impressionistic darned and layered embroidery, leaving some frayed and trailing threads to create movement. I created the outline bird shapes on invisible organza, with a layer of blue shot Mokuba organza ribbon and roughly shaded into these to give a suggestion of starlings in harmony as a murmuration. I overlaid a layer of pale blue Perspex on this backdrop, to give a watery reflective quality.

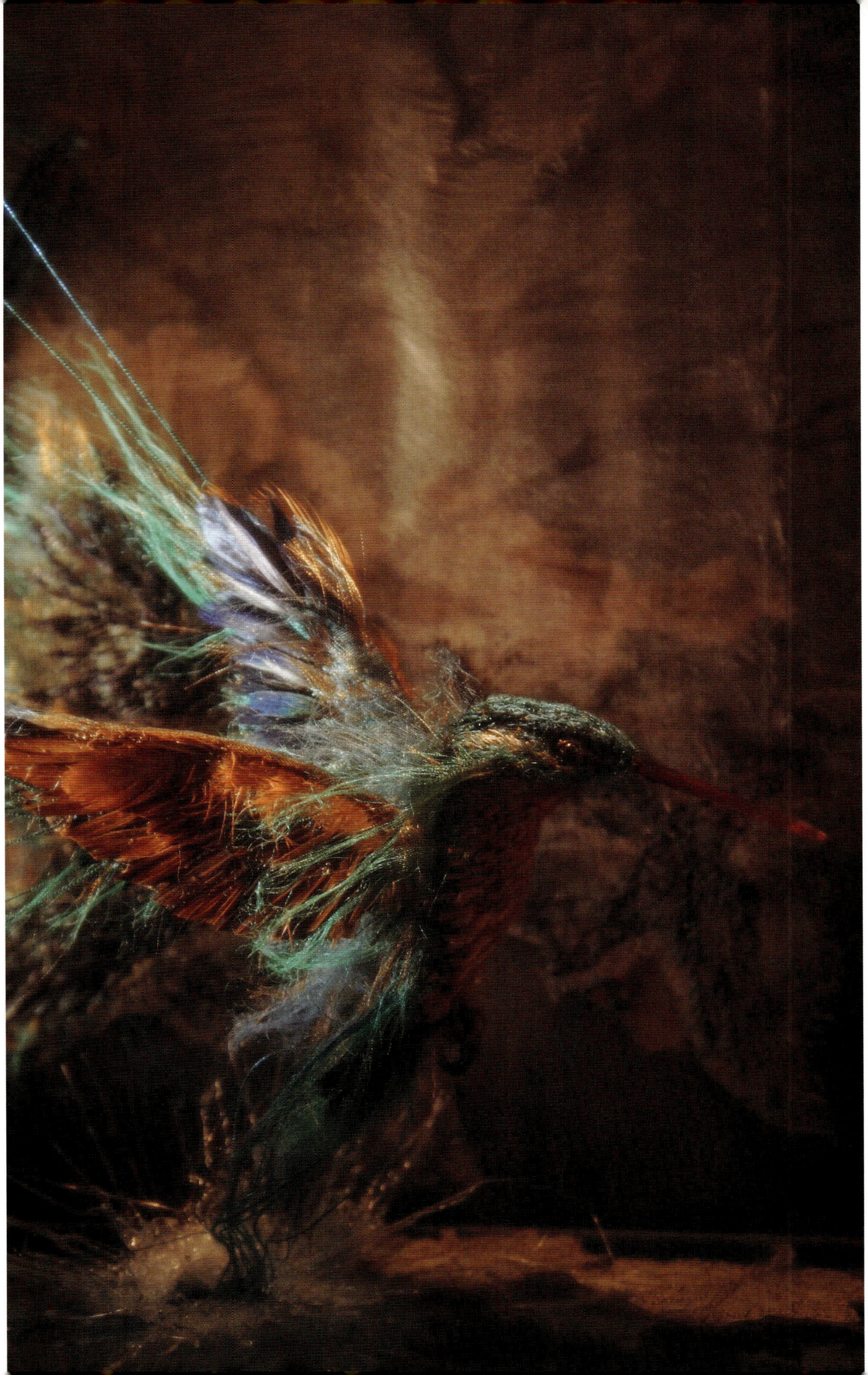

THE KINGFISHER

For the central focus, the kingfisher, I created the initial shape by needle felting and covered this shape with mesh wire. Wanting to create this as an impressionistic piece, trying to capture the essence of movement in the bird, I chose to darn into and stitch small patches of embroidered feather onto the body, leaving some trailing threads. I added some frayed organza ribbon, again leaving these ends trailing to enhance the illusion of movement. I made the beak using the end of a feather quill, and the wings were constructed from a needle-felted base, with mesh wire over, embroidered feather detail, and frayed organza ribbon layers. I then inserted small peacock feathers into the wing shape, and orange feathers on the underside. Again, I added some more frayed organza ribbon layers to create the movement.

I haven't been fortunate enough to catch sight of a kingfisher myself, but have heard accounts when listening to the radio that express the excitement, sheer joy and delight that such an encounter provokes, and I wanted to capture this somehow. I imagined this bird taking flight, emerging from the water, flashing across the sky, so I wanted to create a base that gave the impression that this kingfisher had burst from the water below.

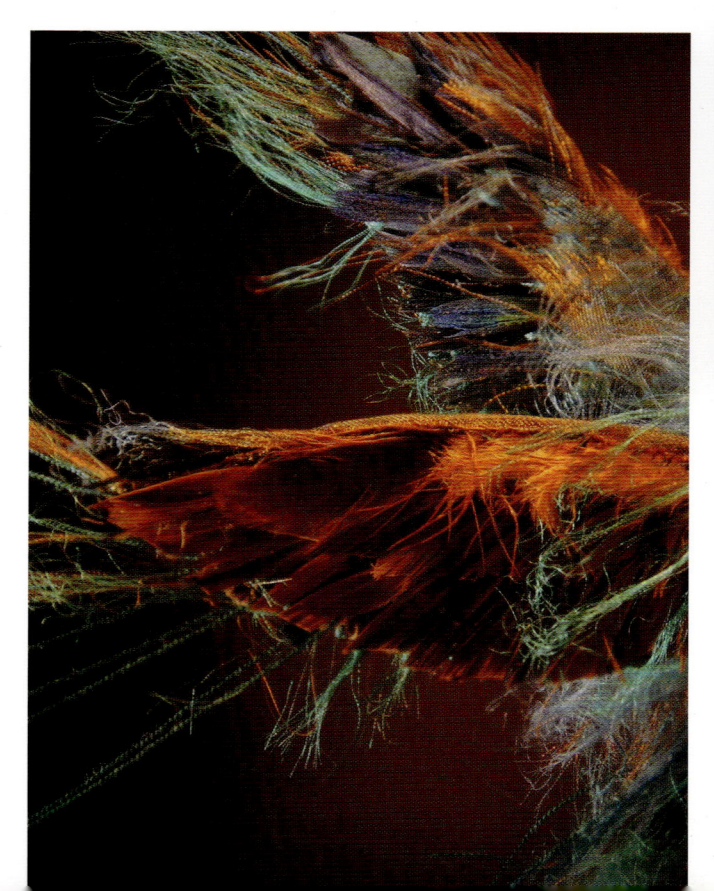

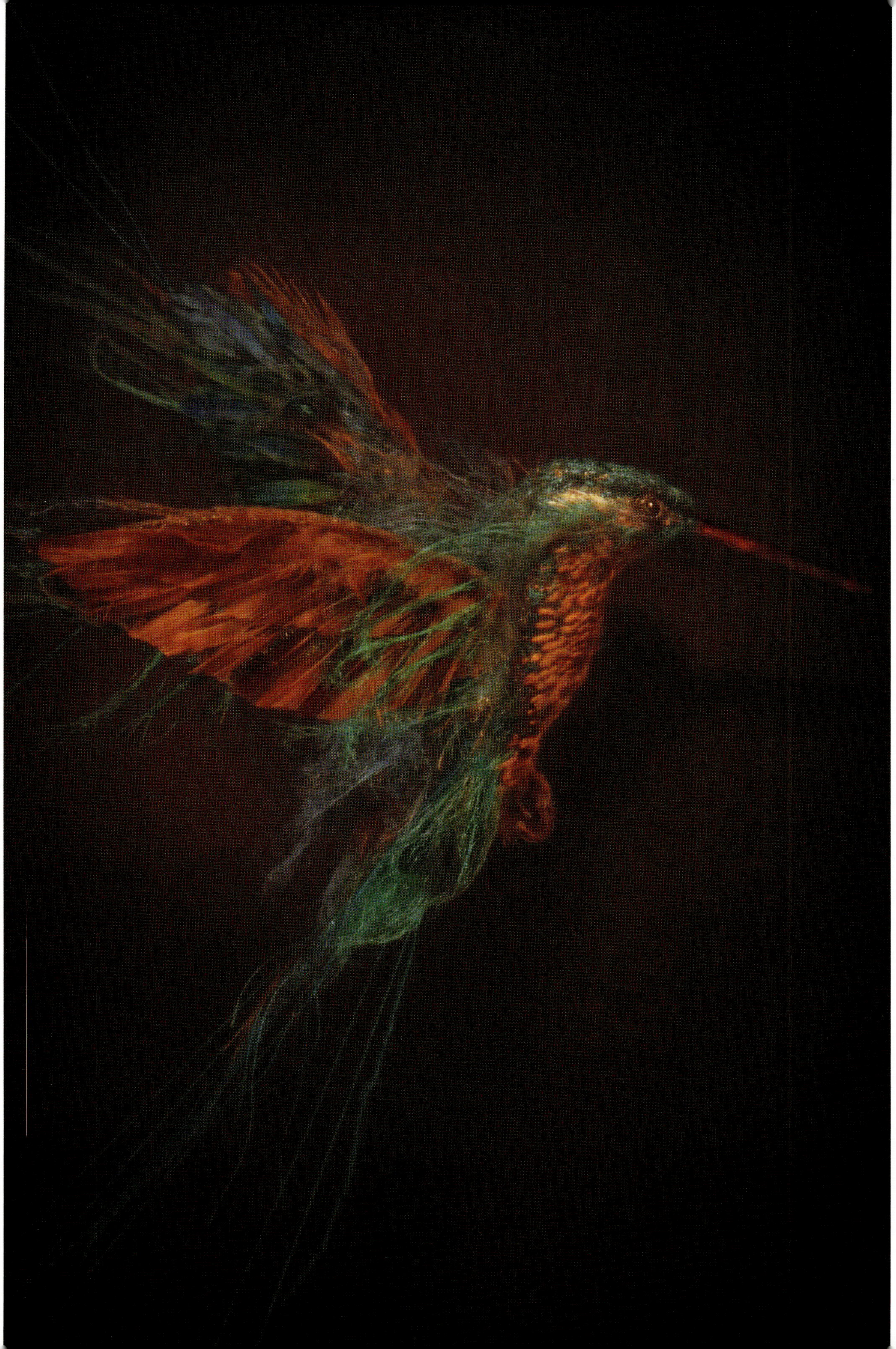

WATER BASE

I created some sycamore leaves with an outline stitch on grey invisible organza and backed them with mother-of-pearl veneer to create a shadow leaf pattern (see left).

For the water base I laid down some blackened bronze silver leaf on Perspex and painted over it with rust-effect paint. I then used a piece of pale blue Perspex as a top layer, onto which I would create the splash. I drilled a series of small holes into the Perspex in a roughly circular shape and then used a hammer and flat-head screwdriver to tap out the hole. I also tapped into the edges of the hole to create cracks in the Perspex and then glued the small pieces of Perspex that come off when you drill it onto the edges of the hole, along with some blue diamond waste bangle cuts that are reminiscent of small bubbles in the water. I used some crystal matchstick points to create another layer of the breaking water. I couched these down onto grey illusion tulle and then glued over the stitches on both sides to hold them in place, before giving them a light wash of blue ink.

On a visit to the 4D Model Shop, I happened to see a display showing some samples created using a three-dimensional printing pen. One of these was a really beautiful sculpted dinosaur in clear filament. I thought this may work for the splash of water I needed for the kingfisher, so I played around with the pen and created some random shapes. I built these together to create my desired effect, then I gave them a light wash of blue ink (see below left).

I wanted this artwork to give a rough, painterly impression that is mirrored in a dark abyss, capturing a fleeting moment that changes in an instant; the darkness broken by a tiny flash of blue and orange streaking into consciousness, awakening the senses and making the heart soar.

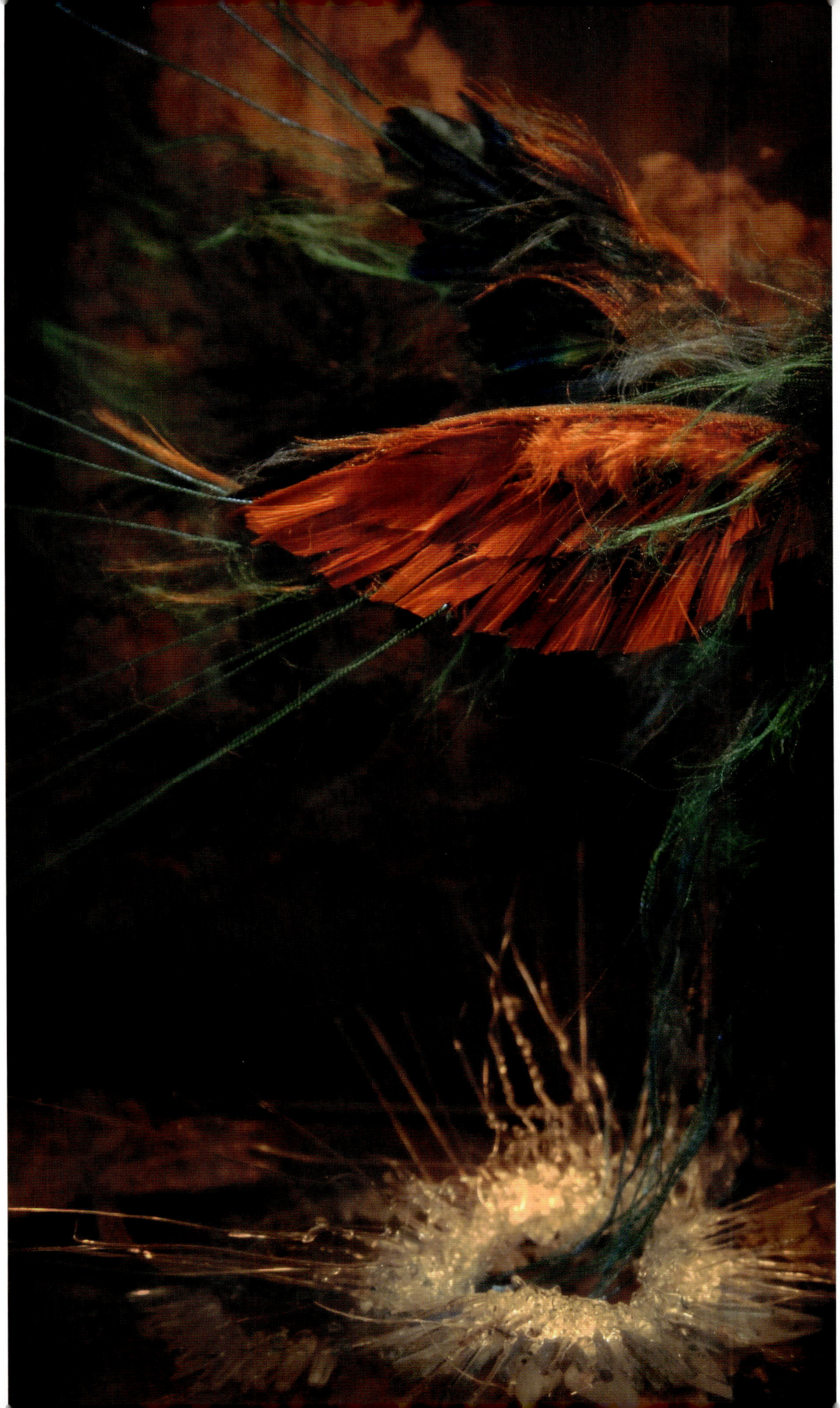

"I see the world being slowly transformed into a wilderness: I hear the approaching thunder that, one day, will destroy us too. I feel the suffering of millions. And yet, when I look up at the sky, I somehow feel that everything will change for the better, that this cruelty too shall end, that peace and tranquillity will return once more."
Anne Frank

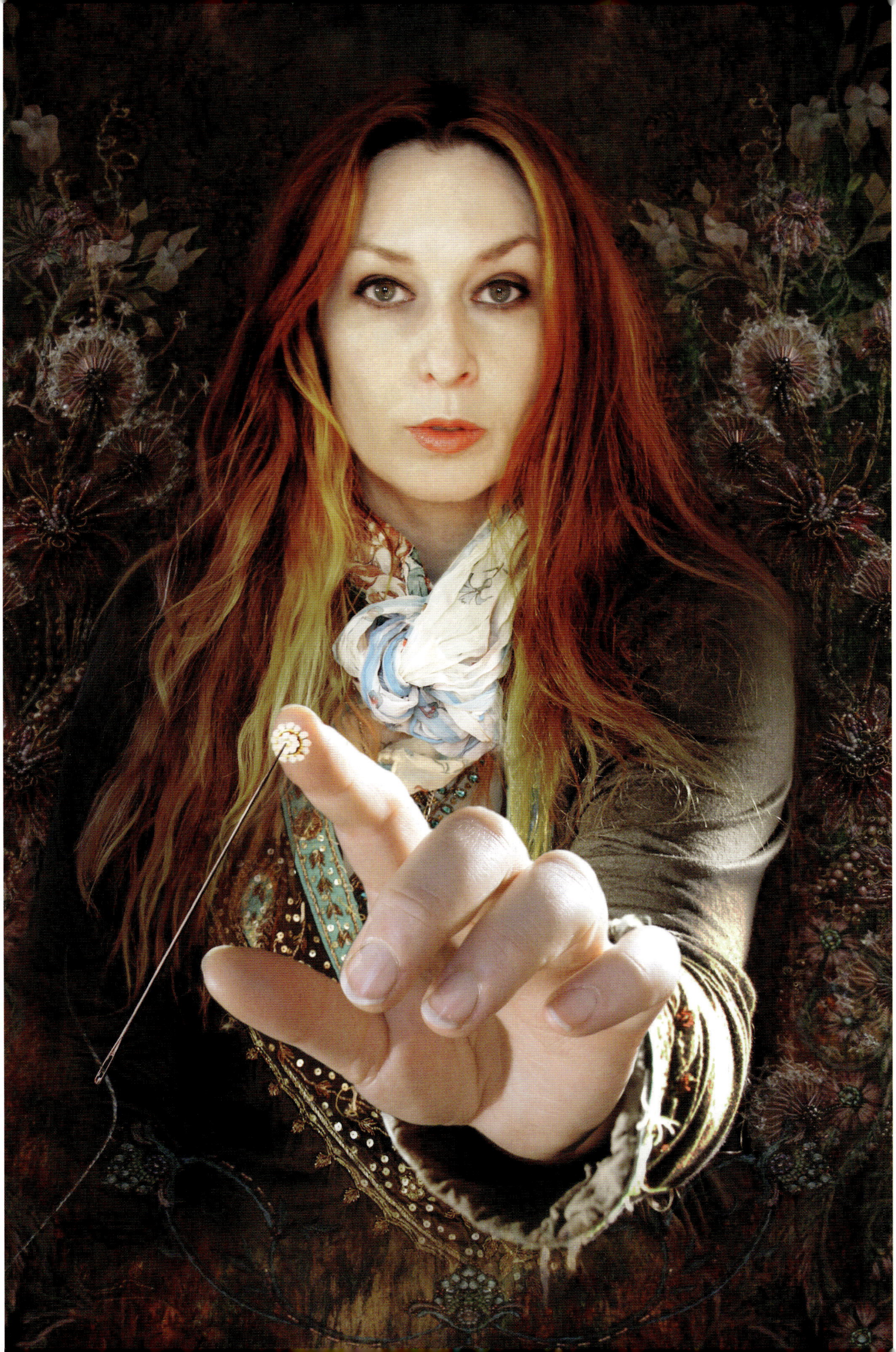

COSTUME

EMBROIDERY

My path into costume work

This final chapter of my book highlights some of my previous work creating embroidery details on costumes for film and TV. Working in this industry is very much a collaborative effort, and I am a small part of a costume team who are all working towards the designer's vision for a particular production. Each costume project is a learning curve and everything helps clarify your approach to the next piece you are asked to create. Each production and each designer may require a differing approach or skill set from you. There will be many ideas from various sources – including the show runners, the director, the writer, other heads of department and the actors – and all of this will be taken into account when the costume designer starts their process. Once the designer has their ideas approved and the fabrics sourced, a small team will start to cut some shapes and toile costumes for initial fittings, as well as sourcing pieces from one of the costume-hire companies; a bit further down the line I may be asked to sample some embroidery or textile-embellishment ideas for specific pieces and everything evolves from there.

Time is always something you need to have in the back of your mind – I have to find ways of producing a design that won't hold up the costume maker's process, as the style, shape and fit is of most importance. After I have created some embellishment, it may need to go to the team of breakdown artists, who will carefully age and distress various costumes as the project requires, so I need to have in mind that they also need time to work their magic.

There are many people like myself working within the costume department. Much of the decorative work is done by the costume makers, who add trims and extra stitching or beading, but there are also textile artists using free-motion machine embroidery with some hand stitching, some using computerized machine embroidery and others using traditional hand embroidery methods.

Because of the success of *Game of Thrones* and the nature of online content-sharing, the work that I and other craftspeople do has been highlighted, which is great to show those still studying that there is a whole world out there where they can find a place to utilize their skills. I am often asked how to get into film and TV work, and there isn't really one answer to give – mostly it is word of mouth, as the same teams of people work together from one project to another. It is really important to take any opportunity that crosses your path as you never know where it will lead. I had a meandering path to the work I do today – after leaving college where I studied fashion design, I was given the opportunity to work in textile conservation. I was introduced to Kitty Morris Conservation through a mutual friend, as I had the hand-embroidery skills required for a textile they were restoring, and I have spent many years working with Kitty in between my film work. It is here I really honed my hand-needle skills, building up speed and precision. The work that I have done with Kitty has been invaluable to my work in film and TV – the materials, techniques and inspiration from all the textiles that have passed through my hands have all contributed to my costume-embroidery development.

My first forays into the filming world were with a group of friends who made short art films, and I helped out in the costume department on these productions. Through one of these friends, who was working on a low-budget feature film, I was enticed along to see if I could help out, and I was very fortunate to be introduced to Mike O'Neill, the costume designer on the production. Mike was a very experienced designer who had worked on many award-winning period dramas, and after this initial job I went on to work with him on many other projects, where he became a great mentor to me. Mike became aware of my sewing skills and gave me little makes or embroideries to do on each job we worked on. This saw me progressively moving away from costume assisting to the making and embellishing of costumes, and he gave me my first role as Principal Costume Embroiderer on HBO's mini-series, *Elizabeth 1*. The work I have done with Mike and my conservation work have been integral to my further development as an embroidery artist.

Alongside the work I did with Mike, I was also introduced to another costume designer, Mary Jane Reyner, who had a small costume-hire business in East London to coincide with her design work. Initially I did some illustrations for her and then started to help out at the costume-hire business. I did some daily on-set assisting and made many prop-costumes and embroidery pieces for her, again being allowed to develop from project to project. It is really good to work with different designers, as each will require something specific from you and help you to expand your knowledge and skills for future collaborations.

A few years later I was introduced to the costume designer Michele Clapton, and I worked with her on various TV shows, creating embroidery details, and also making decorative reticules and fans. So when she was asked to do the pilot for *Game of Thrones* she already had some ideas in mind for me to work on. When working on a pilot there is no guarantee that the show will be commissioned, so at the beginning, no one knew if we would continue to create the whole series. As luck would have it for all of us involved, it was a success, and many continued to work on all eight seasons of the show. I do realize I have been very fortunate to work on a long-running show like this with Michele at the helm, as I have been given an opportunity to experiment and develop my skills from season to season and, as it was a fantasy, was not restricted to one period or style.

Some of the productions I have worked on have been kind enough to allow me to include a selection of images of the embroidery I have created for various costumes. When I work on each costume embroidery I document my process, as sometimes I need to create doubles of a design and may not have access to the original or a prototype sample to refer to; these images become my bible to work from. I wanted to include some of my costume embroidery to show how this has enabled me to develop my skills and how it has been part of my path to the artwork I have created for this book.

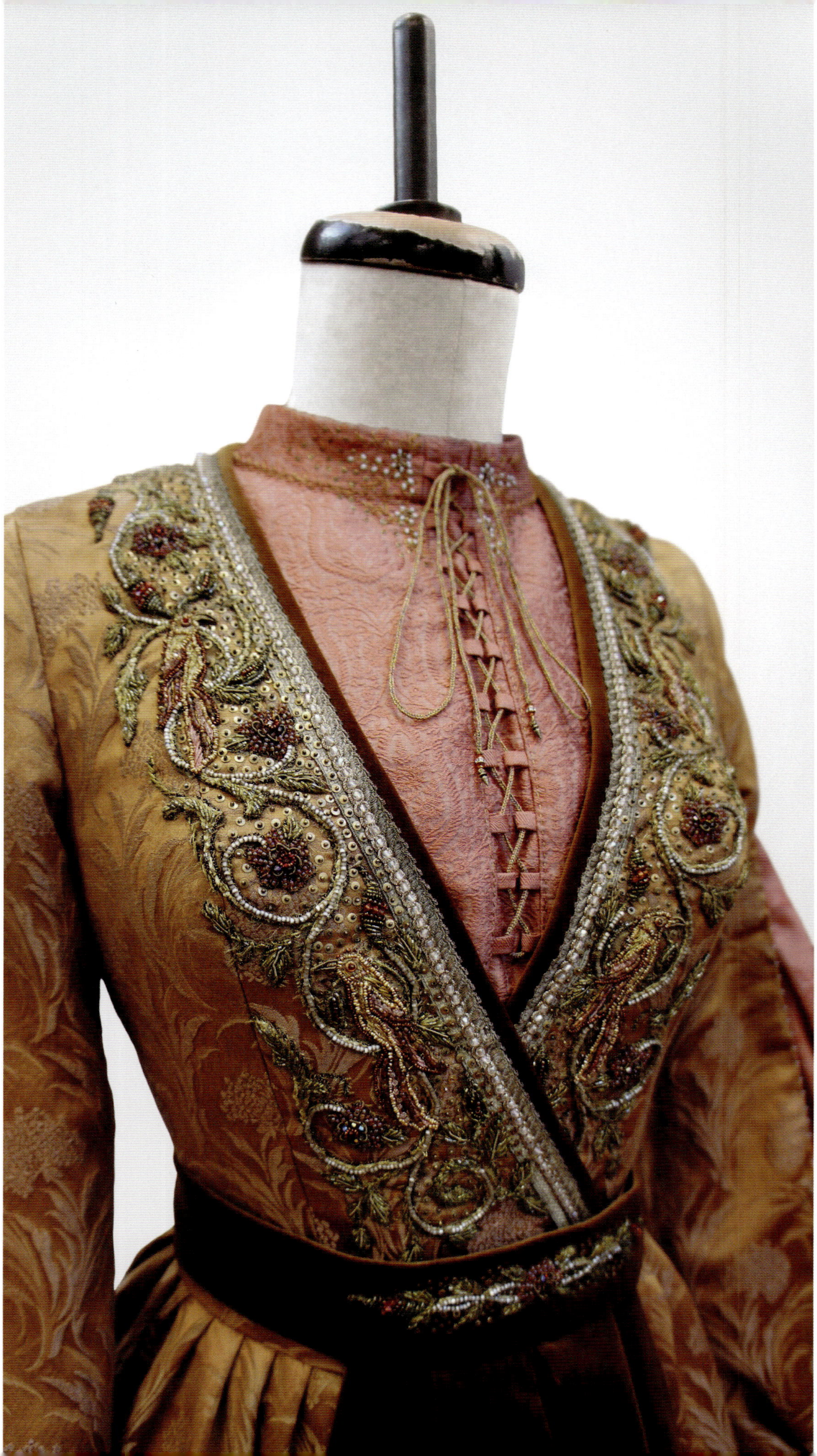
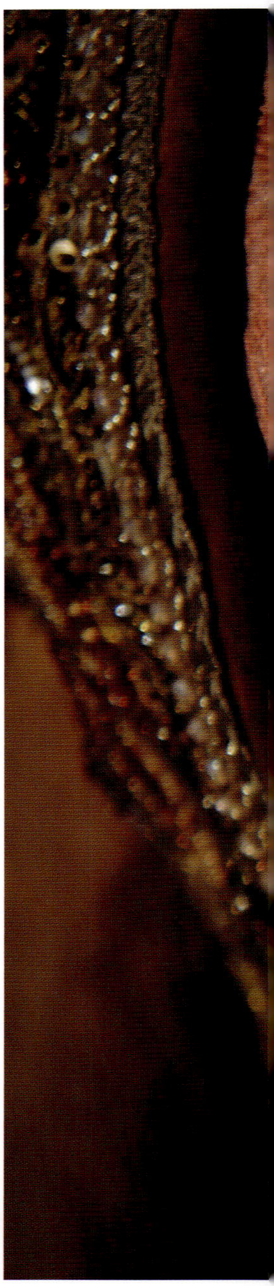

INSIGHT

This piece was designed to give the impression of a traditional Georgian costume. It features freshwater pearls, silk satin Miyuki beads and gemstones. The costume was cut and made by Christine Atkinson.

OPPOSITE: *traditional costume from Ali & Nino; PeaPie Films/Archery Pictures, 2016; costume designer Michele Clapton; photograph © MCE*

ABOVE: *traditional costume from Ali & Nino; PeaPie Films/Archery Pictures, 2016; costume designer Michele Clapton; photograph © MCE*

LEFT: opera coat from Ali & Nino; PeaPie Films/Archery Pictures, 2016; costume designer Michele Clapton; photograph © MCE

ABOVE: opera coat cuff from Ali & Nino; PeaPie Films/Archery Pictures, 2016; costume designer Michele Clapton; photograph © MCE

OPPOSITE: opera coat collar from Ali & Nino; PeaPie Films/Archery Pictures, 2016; costume designer Michele Clapton; photograph © MCE

INSIGHT

This green velvet opera coat has peacock and feather motifs embroidered on the cuffs and collar. It features synthetic opals, crystals and French steel cut beads. The costume was cut and made at Cosprop.

INSIGHT

This purple taffeta ballgown was inspired by Charles Frederick Worth. It features a stylized rose briar design embroidered across the bodice, incorporating a velvet rose corsage and beaded stems trailing off to the side. The costume was cut and made by Clare Ramsell.

OPPOSITE: ballgown from *Queen of the Desert*; Benaroya Pictures, 2015; costume designer Michele Clapton; photograph © MCE

ABOVE: ballgown bodice detail from *Queen of the Desert*; Benaroya Pictures, 2015; costume designer Michele Clapton; photograph © MCE

RIGHT: ballgown corsage and bodice detail from *Queen of the Desert*; Benaroya Pictures, 2015; costume designer Michele Clapton; photograph © MCE

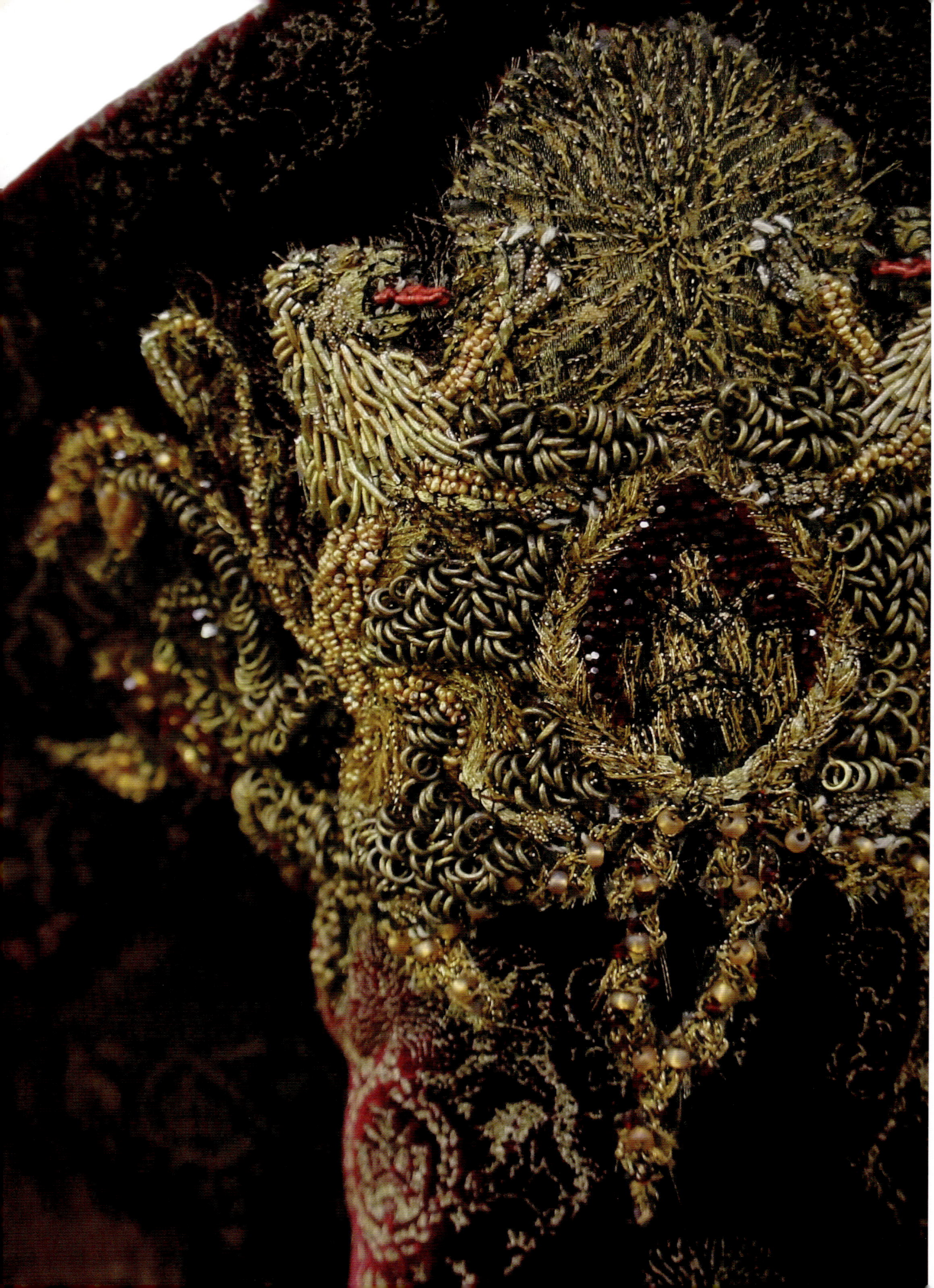

INSIGHT (OPPOSITE)

This hand-printed velvet formal dress features embroidered Lannister House sigil motifs, using tiny freshwater pearls, crystals and jump rings to embellish. The costume was cut by Carole O'Neal.

OPPOSITE: *arm detail from one of Cersei's dresses, season 3, Game of Thrones; HBO Inc.; costume designer Michele Clapton; photograph © MCE*

INSIGHT (RIGHT)

This informal kimono robe features raised embroidery lion heads, in a beaded filigree setting. The costume was cut by Carole O'Neal.

RIGHT: *arm detail from one of Cersei's dresses, season 4, Game of Thrones; HBO Inc.; costume designer Michele Clapton; photograph © MCE*

INSIGHT

This richly textured dress uses smocking techniques, various beads and lock stitch. The costume was cut and made by Margaret Pescott.

LEFT: *one of Daenerys' dresses, season 4, Game of Thrones; HBO Inc.; costume designer Michele Clapton; photograph © MCE*

OPPOSITE: *embroidery details from one of Daenerys' dresses, season 4, Game of Thrones; HBO Inc.; costume designer Michele Clapton; photograph © MCE*

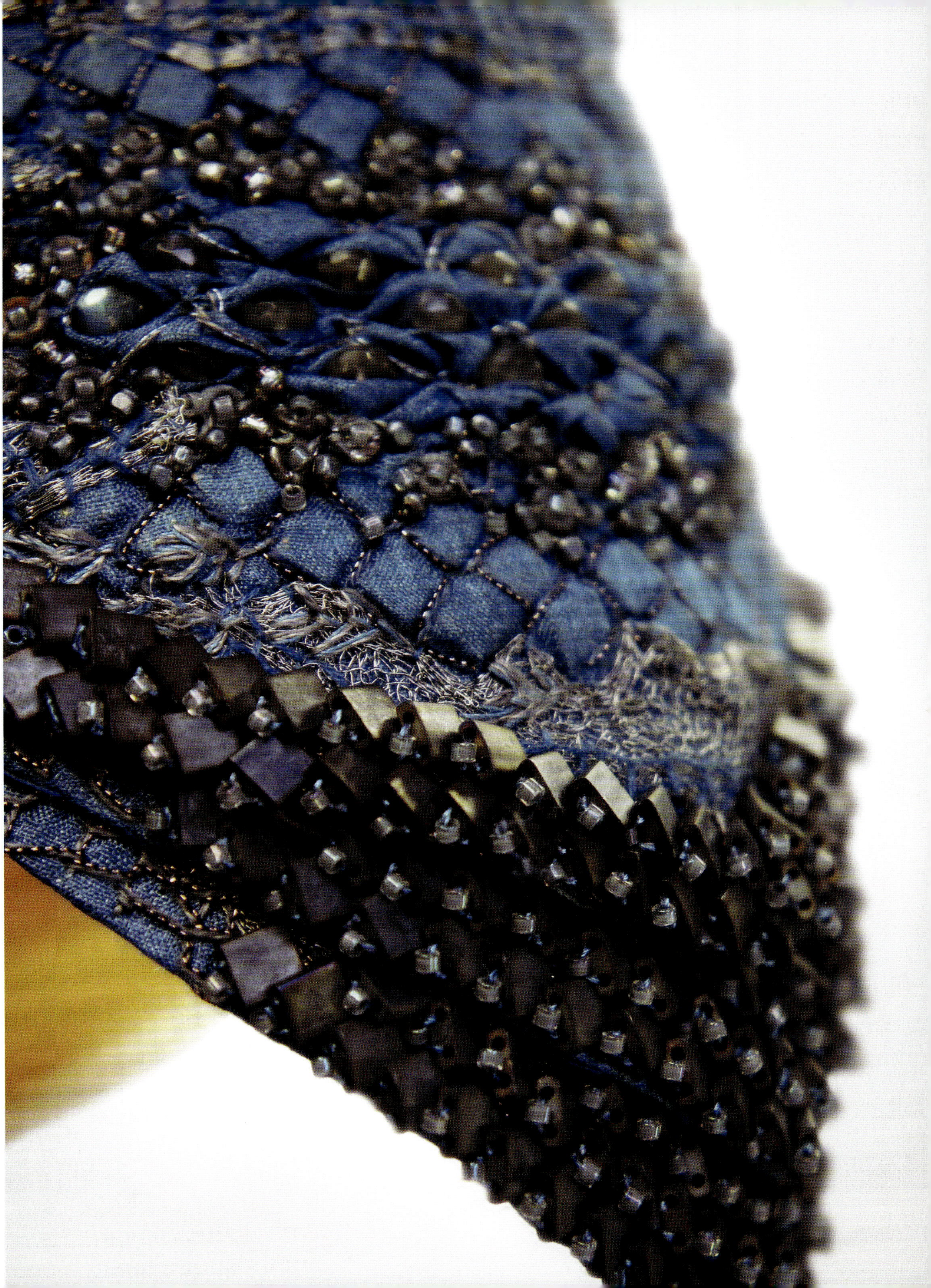

INSIGHT

This is an embroidered interpretation of the Stark family sigil, with the addition of their sacred weirwood tree, growing into, feeding and giving strength to the direwolf. I used mesh wire, various threads, mother of pearl, freshwater pearls, green amethyst and vintage French steel cut beads. The costume was cut by Carole O'Neal.

Embroidery detail from one of Sansa's costumes, season 6, Game of Thrones; HBO Inc.; costume designer April Ferry; photograph © MCE

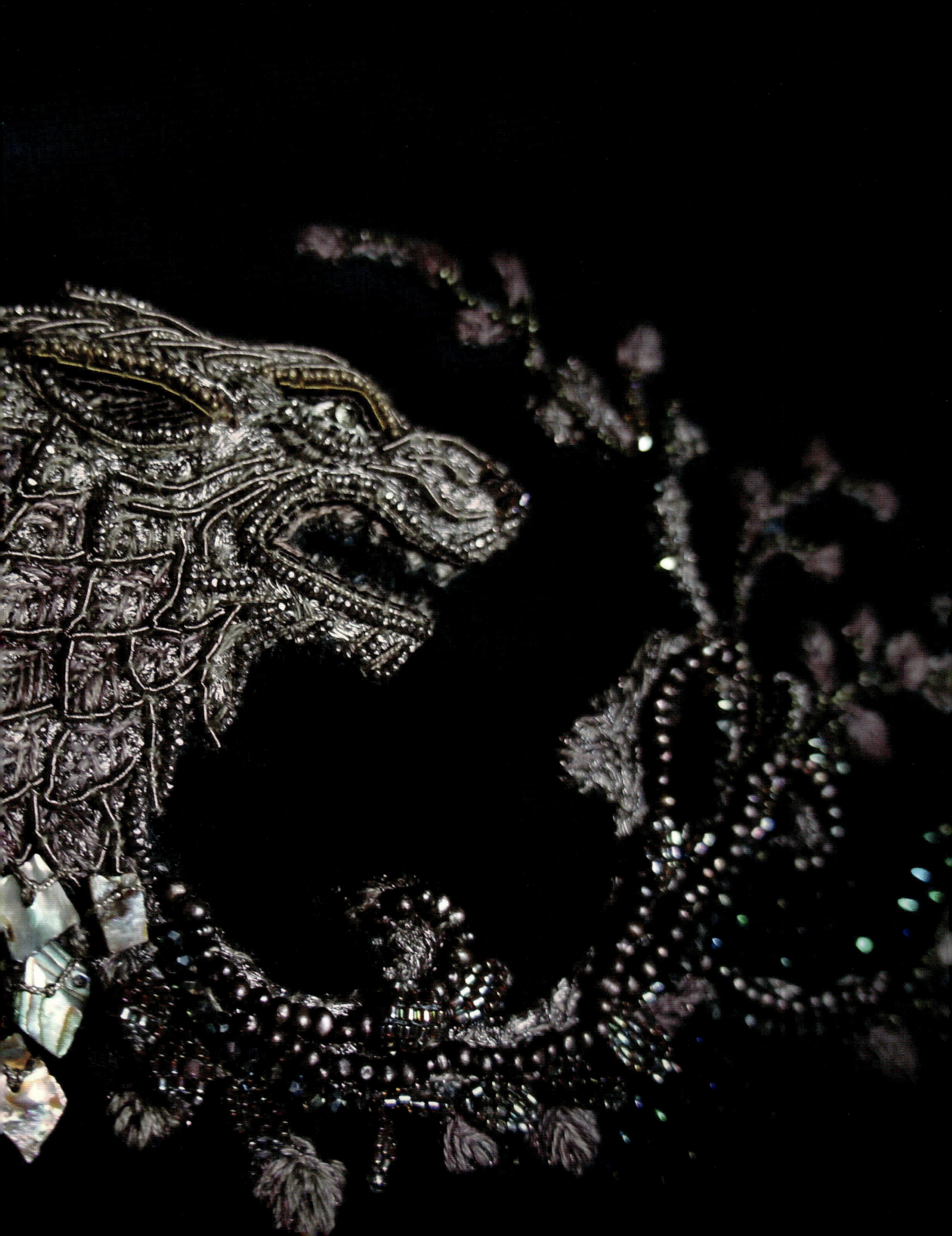

INSIGHT

This embroidered armour consists of a gorget and pauldrons. The costume cutter Carole O'Neal created the base shapes and I made filigree sections that lay on top, adding many braids, beads, crystal spikes and some stumpwork lion heads.

ABOVE: *Cersei's gorget and pauldrons, season 7, Game of Thrones; HBO Inc.; costume designer Michele Clapton; photograph © MCE*

LEFT: Cersei's gorget detail, season 7, Game of Thrones; HBO Inc.; costume designer Michele Clapton; photograph © MCE

BELOW: Cersei's pauldron detail, season 7, Game of Thrones; HBO Inc.; costume designer Michele Clapton; photograph © MCE

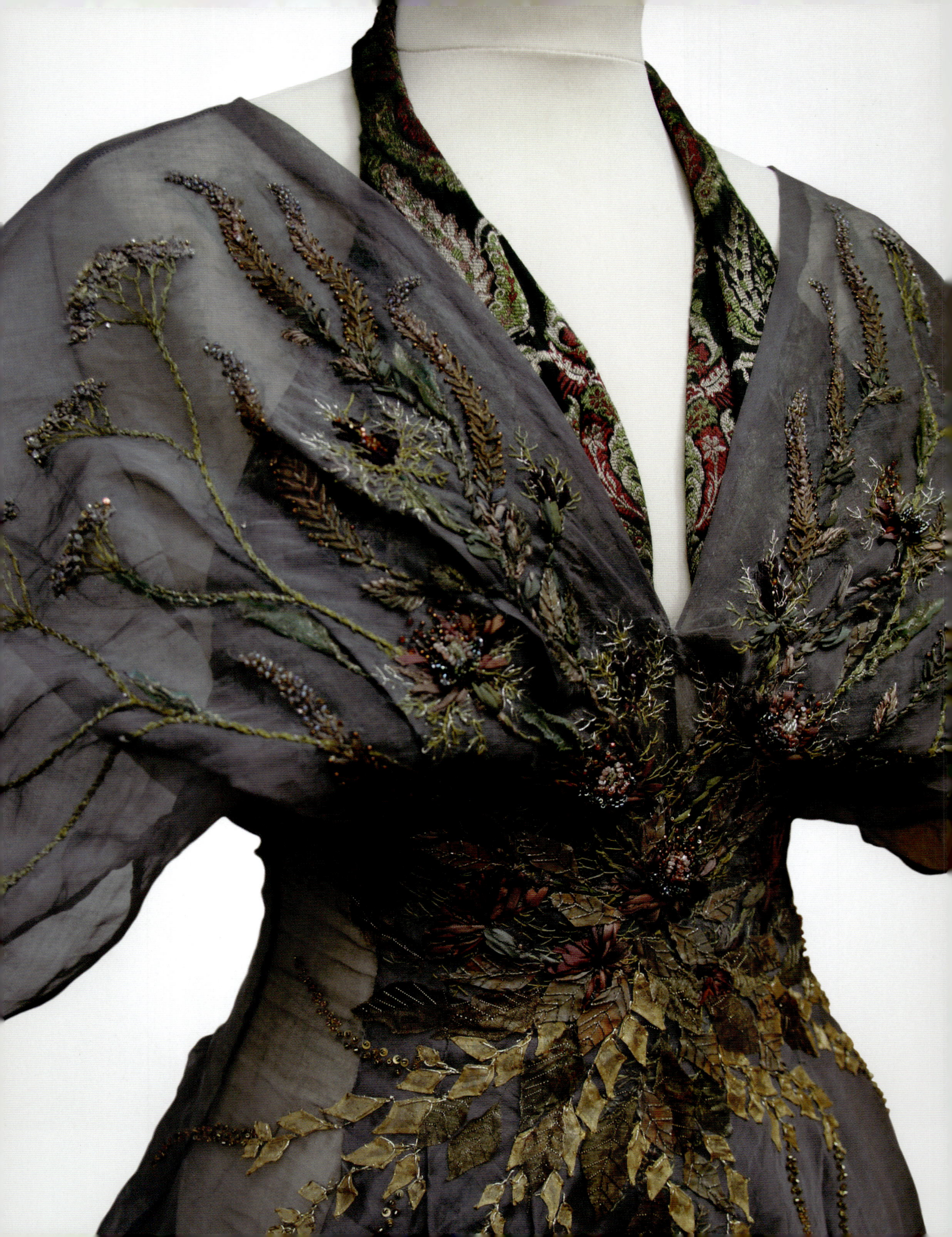

INSIGHT

I used some initial stitching to sketch out the pattern of the flowers on silk crepeline, which was dyed to match the dress, and then embellished with beading and ribbonwork when applying this to it. The costume was cut by Nicki Varney.

OPPOSITE: *bodice detail from Ellaria's dress, season 5, Game of Thrones; HBO Inc.; costume designer Michele Clapton; photograph © MCE*

RIGHT: *embroidery detail from Ellaria's dress, season 5, Game of Thrones; HBO Inc.; costume designer Michele Clapton; photograph © MCE*

INSIGHT

This ethereal dress featured a combination of stitching, ribbonwork and bead embellishment. The costume was cut by Nicki Varney.

RIGHT: *bra embroidery detail from Myrcella's dress, season 5, Game of Thrones; HBO Inc.; costume designer Michele Clapton; photograph © MCE*

OPPOSITE: *bodice embroidery detail from Myrcella's dress, season 5, Game of Thrones; HBO Inc.; costume designer Michele Clapton; photograph © MCE*

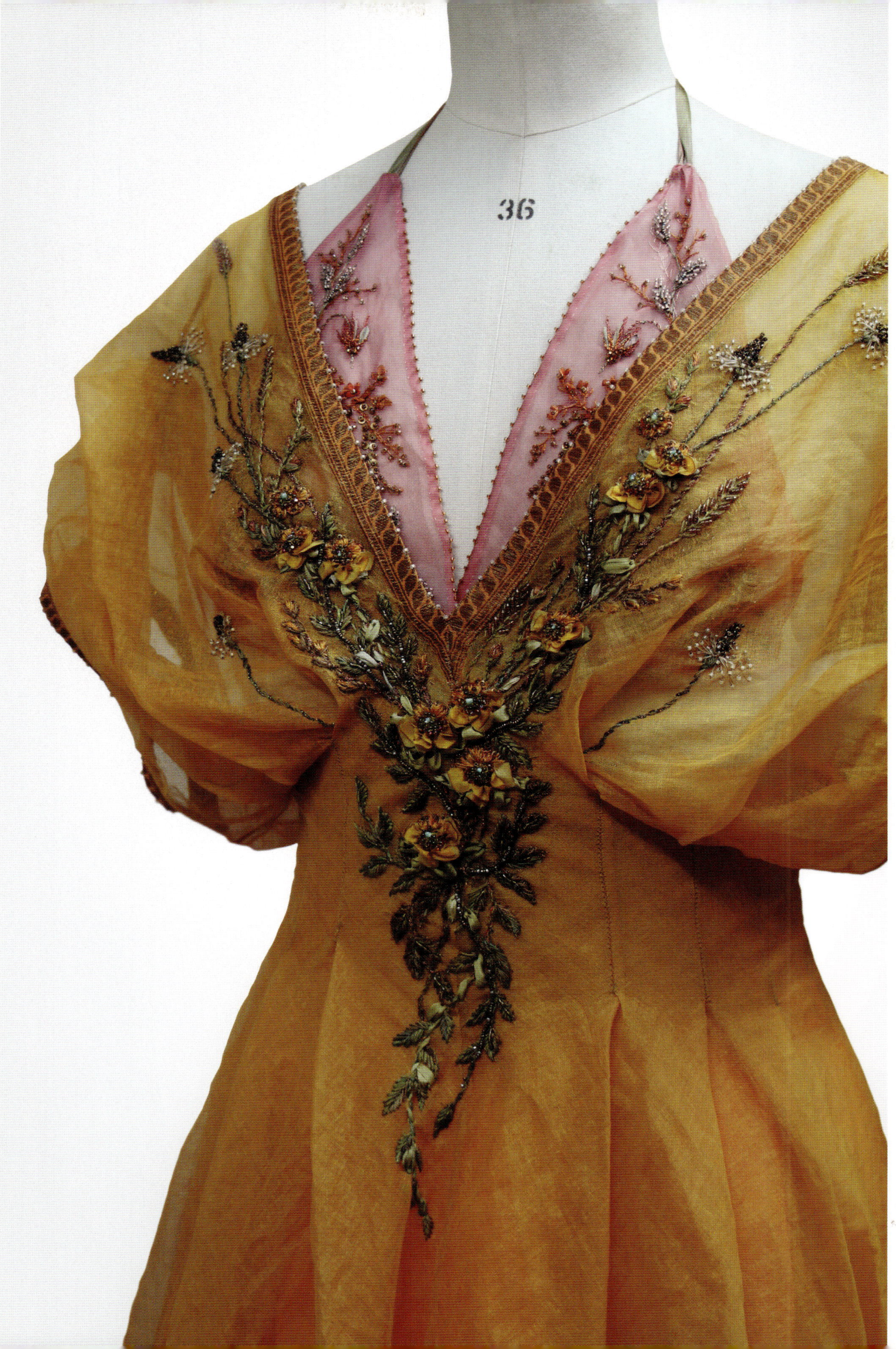
36

INSIGHT

An initial embroidered base design was overworked with ribbonwork, bead embellishment and bead weave petals. The costume was cut by Nicki Varney.

LEFT: bodice detail from Nymeria's bead flower dress, season 5, Game of Thrones; HBO Inc.; costume designer Michele Clapton; photograph © MCE

OPPOSITE: bodice detail from Nymeria's bead flower dress, season 5, Game of Thrones; HBO Inc.; costume designer Michele Clapton; photograph © MCE

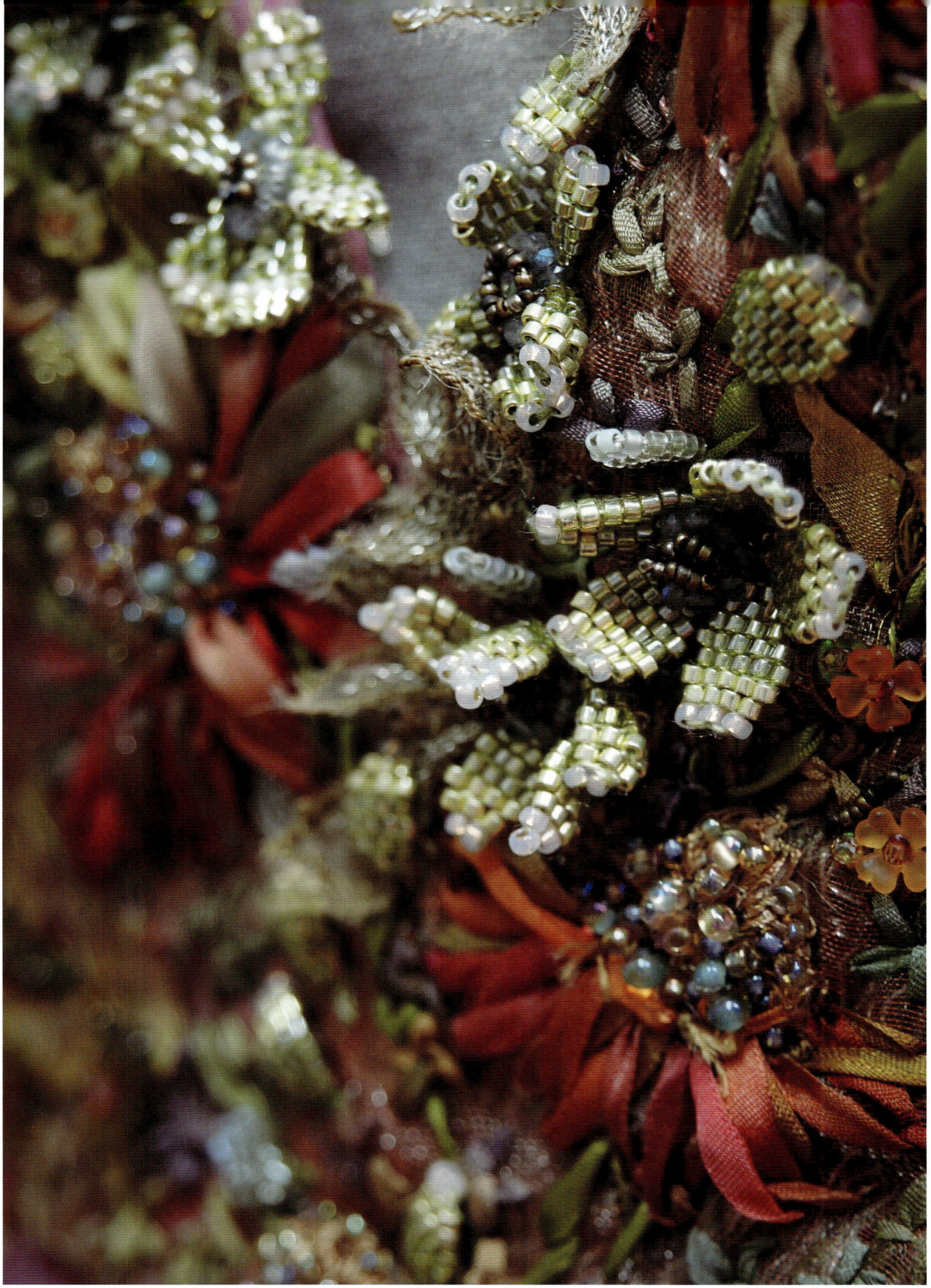

INSIGHT

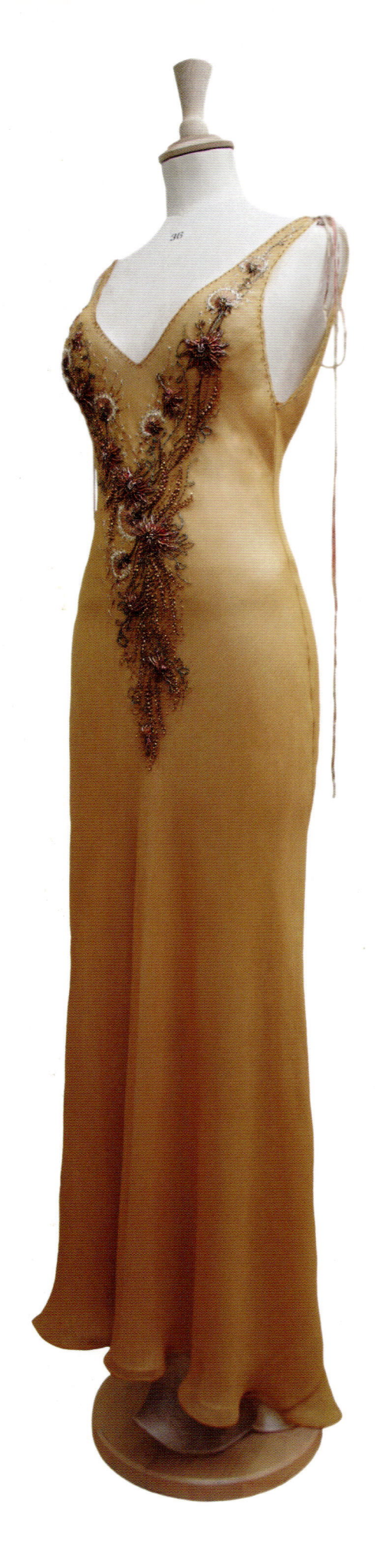

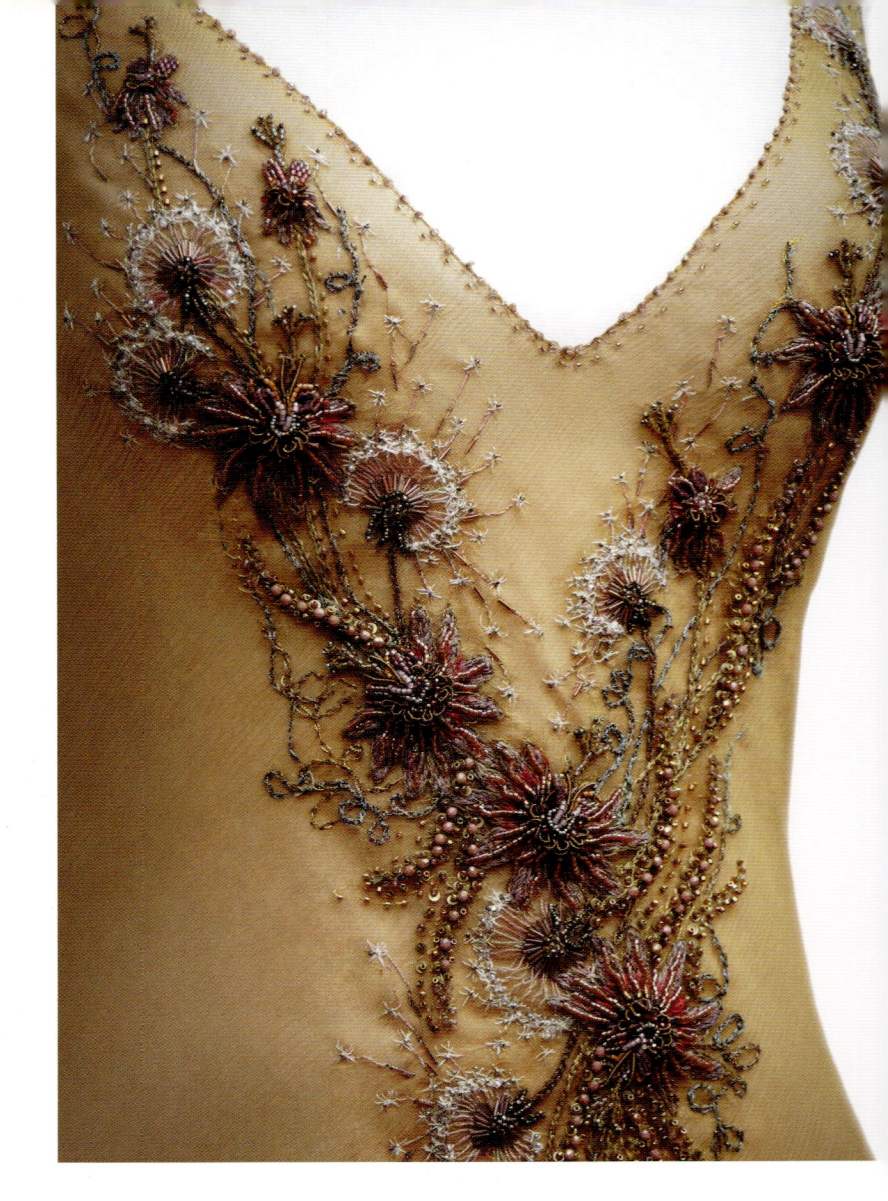

For this bias-cut chiffon dress, I embroidered and beaded on a separate invisible organza base, then applied the design onto the costume, before adding further stitching and beading. The costume was cut by Nicki Varney.

LEFT: Myrcella's bias-cut dress, season 5, Game of Thrones; HBO Inc.; costume designer Michele Clapton; photograph © MCE

ABOVE AND OPPOSITE: embroidery details from Myrcella's bias-cut dress, season 5, Game of Thrones; HBO Inc.; costume designer Michele Clapton; photograph © MCE

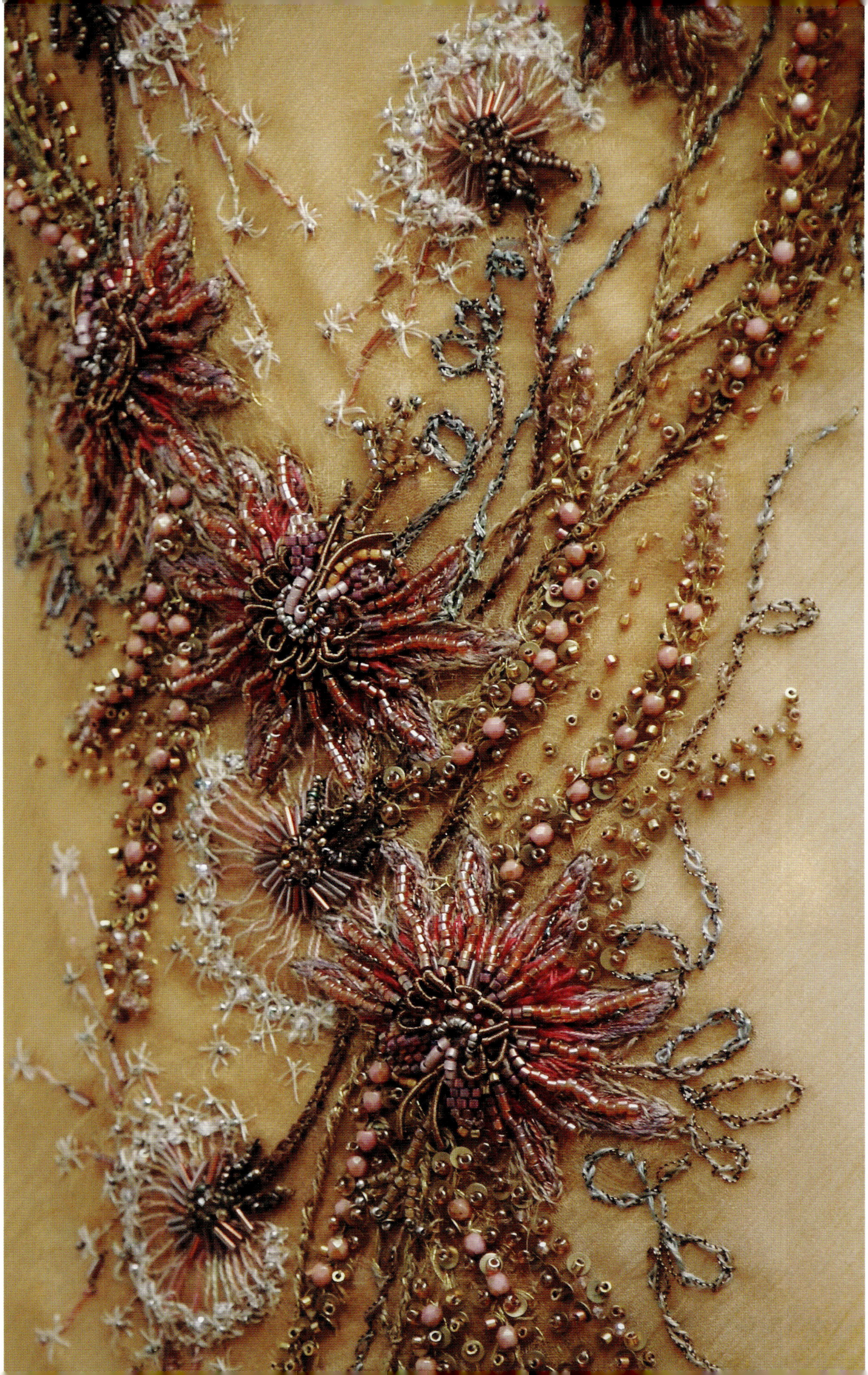

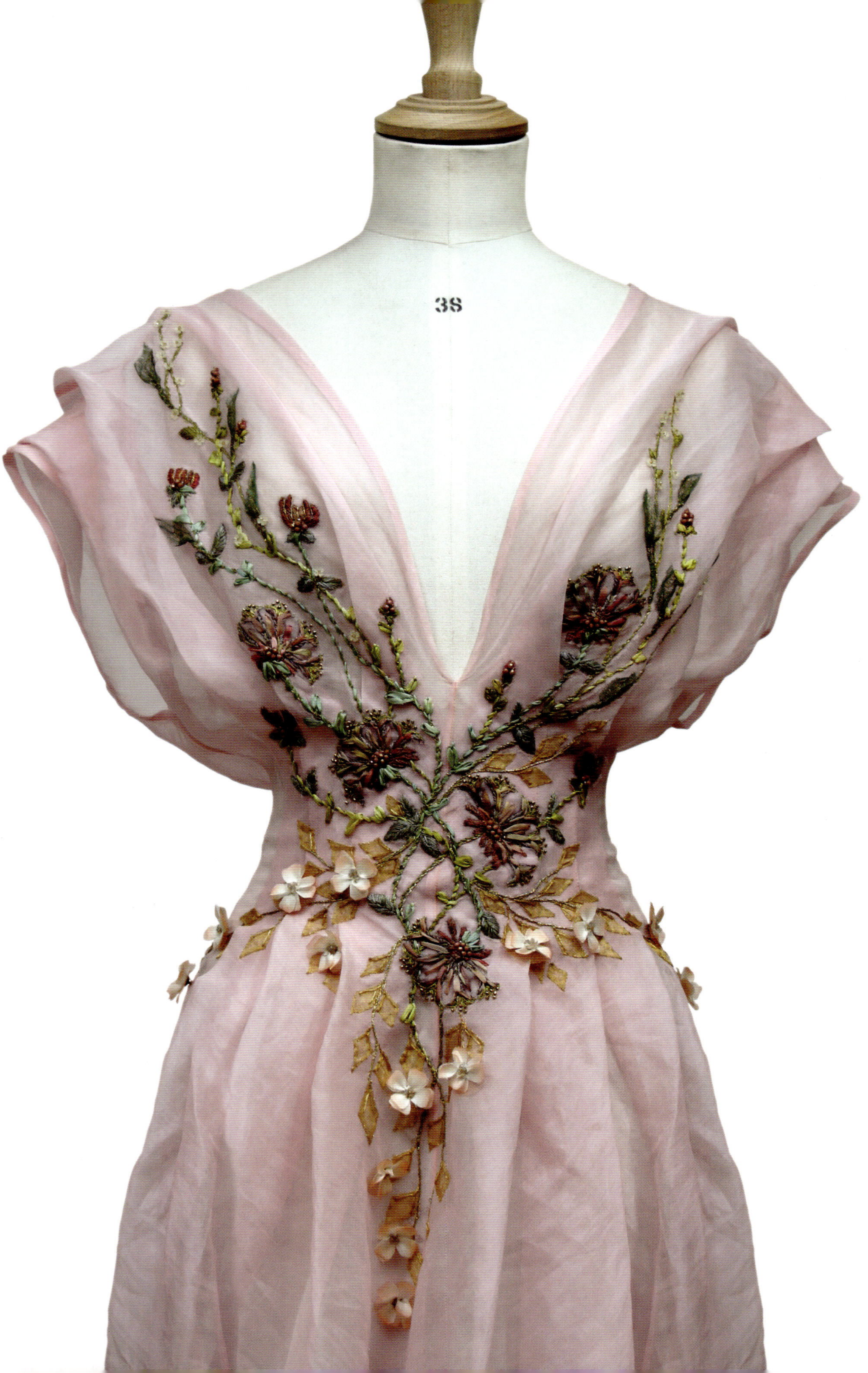
38

INSIGHT

I embroidered the honeysuckle design on silk crepeline dyed to match the dress, and then embroidered into the design as I stitched it to the dress, adding some beading and ribbonwork. Trailing down the front of the skirt and over the hips I added blossom branches; the leaves are made from a metal mesh fabric and each bloom is made with ribbon and small beaded centres. The costume was cut by Nicki Varney.

OPPOSITE: Myrcella's honeysuckle dress, season 5, Game of Thrones; HBO Inc.; costume designer Michele Clapton; photograph © MCE

RIGHT: embroidery detail from Myrcella's honeysuckle dress, season 5, Game of Thrones; HBO Inc.; costume designer Michele Clapton; photograph © MCE

INSIGHT

This was Myrcella's lying-in-state dress. It was similar to her earlier costumes, but darker and more sombre and I wanted the decoration to have the feel of the elaborate chest tombs found in some churches and stately-home chapels.

RIGHT: *bodice detail from Myrcella's lying-in-state dress, season 6, Game of Thrones; HBO Inc.; costume designer April Ferry; photograph © MCE*

OPPOSITE: *lower bodice embroidery detail from Myrcella's lying-in-state dress, season 6, Game of Thrones; HBO Inc.; costume designer April Ferry; photograph © MCE*

171

ABOVE: *jewelled direwolf detail from Sansa's coronation dress, season 8, Game of Thrones; HBO Inc.; costume designer Michele Clapton; photograph © MCE*

RIGHT: *Sansa's coronation dress, season 8, Game of Thrones; HBO Inc.; costume designer Michele Clapton; photograph © MCE*

172

INSIGHT

Sansa's coronation costume – comprising dress and asymmetrical collar – was cut by Carole O'Neal, with armour created by Giampaolo Grassi.

For the direwolf mane I used mother-of-pearl veneer, mesh wire, velvet, hematite beads, vintage silver cord and rabbit fur. The collar is asymmetrical, starting at one side with dark feathers and a small jewelled direwolf head. The fur, as it grows around the collar, turns into a fish-scale pattern, with many shades of velvet embroidered and edged with mesh wire. As the collar sweeps around the shoulders it becomes a sleeve on this side. The velvet scales are trailed off, culminating in beaded embellishment of the woven fabric scale design.

LEFT: bodice and collar details from Sansa's coronation dress, season 8, Game of Thrones; HBO Inc.; costume designer Michele Clapton; photograph © MCE

INSIGHT

Each cuff has the Stark family sigil of a direwolf embroidered on it.

The collar of the dress has a small leaf design embroidered with some chenille detail. At the back of the collar I used the weirwood leaf shapes, embroidered on silk crepeline laid over mother-of-pearl veneer.

The lining of the sleeve has the weirwood tree leaves embroidered with silk and chenille threads, embellished with Swarovski crystals.

ABOVE: sleeve details from Sansa's coronation dress, season 8, Game of Thrones; HBO Inc.; costume designer Michele Clapton; photograph © MCE

LEFT: back-neck embroidery detail from Sansa's coronation dress, season 8, Game of Thrones; HBO Inc.; costume designer Michele Clapton; photograph © MCE

OPPOSITE: inner sleeve detail from Sansa's coronation dress, season 8, Game of Thrones; HBO Inc.; costume designer Michele Clapton; photograph © MCE

*"May the stars carry your sadness away,
May the flowers fill your heart with beauty,
May hope forever wipe away your tears,
And, above all,
May silence make you strong."*

Chief Dan George